HOUSES ARCHITECTS DESIGN FOR THEMSELVES

AN ARCHITECTURAL RECORD BOOK

Edited by   Walter F. Wagner, Jr., AIA
Editor, *Architectural Record*
and
Karin Schlegel

McGraw-Hill Book Company   New York
St. Louis
San Francisco
Düsseldorf
Johannesburg
Kuala Lumpur
London
Mexico
Montreal
New Delhi
Panama
Paris
São Paulo
Singapore
Sydney
Tokyo
Toronto

Library of Congress Cataloging in Publication Data

Wagner, Walter F comp.
    Houses architects design for themselves.

    1. Architects—Homes and haunts—United States.
2. Architecture, Domestic—United States.
I. Schlegel, Karin, joint comp. II. Title.
NA7208.W27   728'.0973   74–2485
ISBN 0–07–002214–3

The editors for this book were Jeremy Robinson and Hugh S. Donlan,
and the designer was Jan V. White.

It was set in Optima by University Graphics, Inc.

It was printed by Halliday Lithograph Corporation and bound
by The Book Press.

34567890 HDBP 798765

HOUSES ARCHITECTS DESIGN FOR THEMSELVES

CONTENTS

iv

PREFACE

When architects design houses for themselves

For many people, houses are the most interesting form of architecture. The reason is simple—of all types of building, houses are the ones closest to the real needs and wants of people, with all the physical and mental complications that word "people" implies.

Houses are intensely interesting to study because each one, in a different way, explores a way of living, and every house—for better or worse—expresses the way of living of the people who have built or bought or rented that house and made it their home.

The basic needs in a house are simple: all of us need a space to sleep, to eat, and to relax. We need bathrooms, and a place to cook food. We need a comfortable temperature. All of the houses shown in this book meet those needs—just as every house, whether it is the lowest-budget apartment or the palatial estate of the wealthiest, meets those needs.

What is important is how those basic needs are met. In all of the 61 houses shown in this book, those needs are met differently; and that is what makes houses fascinating.

A note to readers who bought this book because they are considering a new house (as many readers of this book will be).

You will inevitably look first to see if there are any houses that are just what you are looking for. Chances are you won't find one. You'll find some houses you like, to be sure—ones that suit your ideas of room arrangement, or your idea of what a house should "look like"—whether that is warmly conservative or stark modern. But you almost surely won't find one that is just what you are looking for because the house was not designed with you in mind. It was designed by an architect for his own family—and they do not have the same ideas about their way of living as you have about your way of living.

So while you may be disappointed not to find the house that is "just right for you," I don't think you should be discouraged. I think you should study all of the houses in this book—even the ones you don't like at all—for ideas within each house that please you, that might be incorporated into a different house, a house designed for your family.

Study the various plan arrangements and try and figure out how they work—and why they might work (or not) for your family. Families who do a lot of entertaining need a big living room—sometimes opening off the kitchen to a second entertaining room (familiarly called a family room). But for families where both older children and parents may be entertaining simultaneously, the family room ought to be as far from the living room as possible (unless, of course, you love rock music).

Study the bedroom sizes (indeed, the sizes of all the rooms). In my view, at least, the houses offered these days by many builders are over-scaled. In many architect-designed houses, the bedrooms are quite small, reflecting the obvious fact that most of the time you spend in a bedroom you are asleep and really couldn't care less. Many children (you might ask your own) seem to prefer small rooms, as long as there is space for a desk and for their most important treasures. Space saved in these rooms can (and is, in many houses) traded off into rooms shared by the family.

Note that many of these houses are zoned: into areas for children, areas for parents, and common family areas—each closable from the other (in terms of sound, not just privacy) and that is an important idea for any house.

And notice how almost all of these houses relate to their site. Many builders plunk the house into the middle of the site, and that is that—and in blocks of such builder houses the result is boredom from the street and from the windows of the houses. In contrast, almost all of the houses shown in this book seem to grow from the site, and in many cases (as you'll see in section 1 and in the photos) the design of the house began with the site. That is almost a fundamental precept of architecture, and it is the reason that, so often, custom-built houses offer more than built-for-sale houses.

Look for ideas in the "detailing" of houses —how they are finished—some quite simply and directly, what some people might call "cold and stark," some finished with rich trim and materials. Some use a lot of wood inside for the natural warmth and beauty that universally admired material provides; but many are painted white (surely the architect's favorite color) to provide not just light and cheerfulness, but the best background for handsome furniture and paintings or other wall decoration.

My advice in studying these houses is to look for (I guess the better word is study for) ideas that reflect what you want, perhaps the way you want to live. For a house is (or can be, or should be) perhaps the most personal expression of your life. And it is hard to reach that expression. Writing about his own house (page 210), architect Rem Huygens says: "When an architect designs his own house, I am not sure that he has any more 'free rein' than he has with any client. He can find a personal solution; but if he is at all lucky with his clients, he will be able to find a personal solution for them and himself. And one never really has a 'free rein'; whoever the client, whatever the budget. When designing his own dwelling, in fact, an architect may feel the reins more strongly. He may be his own most demanding client. That these demands can be difficult to satisfy shows in many an architect's own house. When I designed my own house, I was determined to limit these demands. The idea for the house evolved as an abstraction of all the many thoughts I had had over the years about the place where I would live. . ."

"An abstraction of all the many thoughts . . ."—that is what any client must ask for from his architect. Another architect expressed this same bringing-together of ideas: Says Morton Gruber, who designed the house on page 160 for his family: "Before designing my own home, our firm had designed several dozen custom houses aimed to satisfy (as much as possible) a wide variety of residential clients. So I had a mental catalog of desires, goals and objectives that clients wished to achieve. I evaluated these objectives in terms of my own life style—accepting some and rejecting many.

"Designing for one's self and one's own family is truly a soul-searching experience. I feel that the time and effort spent was rewarding and worthwhile in defining an environmental expression of self.

"It has been said that we live only to express ourselves. The expression in its completed three-dimensional form is remarkably fulfilling and satisfying."

There is something very special about a house that is special for you—which is why some people look so hard for houses and don't buy the first fake Colonial that comes along in a town with a good school and a neighborhood with a reputation for good resale value; and why some people (bless them) go and find a good architect and enter on the time-consuming, mind-bending, sometimes frustrating, but always rewarding process of having their own house designed and built just for them. Living in an everyday kind of house—compared with living in a house that really fits your way of living—must be like being married to a woman who has never bothered to learn to cook well; you can get used to it, but you miss something every day of your life.

The design idea for a house can start in a lot of different ways. The editors of this book contacted the architects of each of the houses shown in it, asking them a variety of questions about the design process, what problems they encountered, how the house differed from one they'd do for another client, what they'd do differently if they had it to do over, and whether they still lived in the house and liked it.

**A final word
before you study
the 61 houses
shown in this book. . .**

The editors hope that this analysis of some of the architects' reasons for build-ing, the constraints they accepted, the opportunities they found, and the bene-fits they are enjoying every day will give you a better framework for considering what you might want in a house—now, or sometime.

Significantly, though some of the houses in this book are now over 10 years old—and the average is perhaps four to five—only eight of them are not occupied by their original architect-owners. Of those original owners, three (as can happen to any of us) got in over their heads financially and had to sell their house. But most of the architect-owners of these houses speak of them with pride and love; and more than a few—in one set of words or another—make it clear that this house is *the* house for them—that they intend to live there "from now on."

Which is, whether it works out that way or not, a great way to feel about a house—and a feeling all too rare in these days of houses designed for "average" tastes and needs and for ready resalability.

For what one more voice is worth, this editor has lived in the same house for 18 years and (knock wood) we intend to keep living in it. Eighteen years ago, in our part of Connecticut, you could still find those old houses that young couples could buy cheaply and fix up. When we bought our house I was making one-fourth of my present salary and we had no kids. As we now have four children, needless to say we've added on to the house over the years. The older two (with a little luck and assuming we hit the lottery) will be off to college soon; but we'll find a new use for the space. The house was never too small, and will never be too big, simply because we couldn't think of selling it. Which is a nice way to feel about a house. After 18 years, except on the blackest days, I still actively enjoy driving up to the house. Which is a long-winded way of saying: If you're considering a new house, look hard for the right house. Perhaps you can find it ready and waiting. But if you can't, find yourself a good architect. Together, find a good site. And then build a house that will please you. Then live, as they say, happily ever after.

—Walter F. Wagner Jr.

1

The most frequent answer as to where the design started: the site.

Here are some quotes from architects that express ways of thinking that any prospective homeowner might work through in his mind. They each express a thought that is critical to any really great house: It starts with the land.

Wrote architect Joseph Schiffer of his house on page 144: "The secluded, end-of-road site with a tall stand of pines, pond, and small open meadow were dominant in our thinking about the location and form of the house. It was our choice to work with a simple, quiet, passive enclosure to sublimate the house to the richness of this particular site; and in this sense we feel that we have been able to sense a variation of life outdoors, sun to shade, open to closed, with maximum exposure to the outdoors."

John Carden Campbell says of his house on page 28: "We began with a very small (60- by 80-foot) and very steep site with a spectacular view. The city required two car spaces, and our budget called for building as inexpensively as possible. So the two-car garage was dug into the hill, the bedrooms were put on top of that, and the big living room—with a high, 12-foot, ceiling—was put on top to capture the view." A simple, direct approach.

Steep sites, often overlooked even in built-up areas because they can be difficult to build on, are frequently bought by architects for their own use. There are three reasons: 1) often, they have a view; 2) often, they are less expensive than easy-to-build-on land; and 3) they offer chances for striking and innovative design (and this innovation often makes it possible to build, without great financial penalty, a special solution that a merchant builder would not or could not spend the time working out). Architect Eberhard Zeidler writes movingly of the benefits of working with such sites and the resulting house (page 32) for his family: "Toronto is blessed with ravines which successfully withstood the growth of the city and left a green lace through the city. Our ravine is in the heart of the city. In 1917 a stone house was built into a ledge of the slope, putting the front door 65 feet below street level . . . I left the old stone walls and window openings and used them as the adult part of the house . . . The space is full of hidden surprises, details and changes of mood, from a protected 'cave' space to a four-story view into the sky . . . The new extensions to the house grew into the hill . . . The roof is important, since from the street it is the only part of the house that can be seen. I therefore used it as a strong design element that echoes the uses within the house . . . All roofs are wooden decks, creating a feeling of terraces cascading down the hill . . ."

When a site has a view, inevitably good design must make the most of it. Architect Rodney Friedman writes of how his house (page 20) takes advantage of a magnificent view from a steep site overlooking San Francisco Bay: "The east wall of the house enjoys an abundance of morning sun but a shortage of afternoon sun, and the best views are to the south. Thus, skylights and a glass-roofed and glass-walled part of the living room are placed in order to take advantage of the light, and the marine views in the foreground and the distance. Every room enjoys a view either to the south or east. Native stands of oak, eucalyptus, and pine are preserved on the site so that a mature and established character is maintained. Many design solutions were explored prior to the commitment to this design . . ."

While some houses are "built into" the site, some architects set the simplest geometric shape onto a site; aiming not to blend with the land, but to set the house apart in a respectful way. One example, expressed by architect Jack Freidin about his house (page 26): "The basic idea of the house was to create the simplest possible form which would have minimal interference with the site—a pure geometry floating over the landscape and complementing it. Since we wanted to enjoy the ever-changing surrounding woodland—and since privacy was no problem—I designed a glass-walled living-dining area. It is a delightful experience in every season and in all kinds of weather, day and night (thanks to floodlights which illuminate the trees). We can sit in our living room and see the woodland birds a few feet from us, squirrels, an occasional rabbit or raccoon, and—a number of times each winter—a few deer."

The houses mentioned here, as well as others in the pages of this book, all reflect perhaps the most basic of design approaches—start with the site.

SECTION A-A

The Blum House

Does an architect who has been mainly involved in large-scale work approach residential design differently from one who has only done small buildings? In the case of Sigmund Blum's design for his own house, the answer appears to be yes. What appears to be another modish wood "tower" house in fact has a dazzlingly clear steel structure that seems to come directly from Blum's long experience as chief designer for a large Detroit firm. Yet there is no confusion of scale; for its size the interior is remarkably intimate.

Having found—in the built-up neighborhood where he had lived for many years—a steep-sided vacant lot that was considered unbuildable, he approached the siting with authority. Instead of a scheme using posts or uneven foundations, Blum excavated the triangular portion of earth shown in the section (left). Then, using a two-story retaining wall, he created a horizontal platform on which he erected a steel frame supported by four columns. Masonry wing walls (plan overpage), 28 feet apart, reinforce the retaining wall and provide shear support for the columns. The masonry tubes for stair and elevator stiffen the structure and the frame construction atop the uppermost steel floor. The entire building was then sheathed in 1 by 4 cedar boards. That visual unity contrasts dramatically with the bold overhangs at either end of the top floor.

Thus, in an extremely compact form, Blum has accomplished his two siting goals: to have the house from the downhill side (at right) appear to rise firmly from the earth and from the uphill side (left) to match the scale of the neighboring traditional wood houses. By placing the long dimension of the house across the contours, he also avoided cutting any of the mature spruce trees, including one which helps hide the house from the road.

Architects: Sigmund F. Blum and Harturun Vaporciyan of Blum, Vaporciyan and Mitch, Inc. *Owner:* Sigmund Blum. *Location:* Franklin, Michigan. *Engineers:* Veral Memduh (structural), Jack Meek (mechanical). *Contractor:* Dennis Rouix.

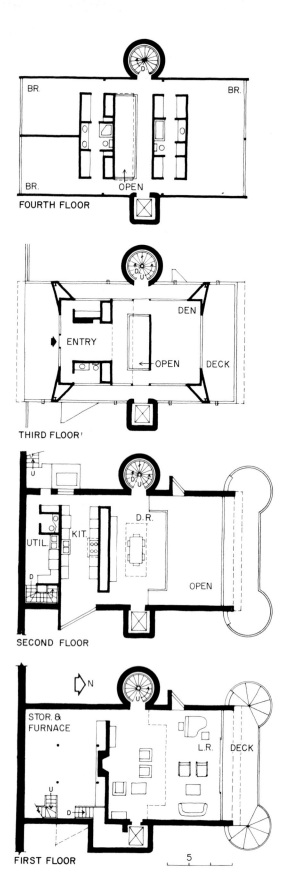

FOURTH FLOOR

THIRD FLOOR

SECOND FLOOR

FIRST FLOOR

Communication between floors in the Blum house is facilitated by the elevator and by the slot in each floor. "We installed an intercom," says the architect, "but no one ever uses it. We just holler." From the entry level, one can look up to the skylight and down past the dining room to the living room floor—quite a surprise to anyone who thought he was approaching a two-story house when he drove in. Another surprise is the clear-span glass wall in the living room, across-page. What appears to be a single pane the width of the room is four pieces of polished plate glass butted and caulked with a transparent elastomeric sealant.

The Brandes House

A narrow, sloping site with a condemned three-story building already on it was bought by Mr. and Mrs. Brandes mainly for its magnificent view over Long Island Sound to the opposite shore of Westchester County. After careful consideration of the problems and advantages of the site, it was decided to pull down the old structure and to erect a completely new house using the old stone foundation, which was in good condition and located at the higher end of the plot. This left the rest of the site free for a terraced garden and enabled the new building to be oriented toward the view.

In order to take full advantage of the view, and to shut out the two large houses on either side, Gina Brandes used as few windows as possible, relying mainly on the glass wall at the north overlooking the Sound, and a plastic bubble skylight in the dining area. One or two small windows are included to give adequate cross ventilation. The living room leads directly onto a lightly supported, screened deck, which is angled away from the nearest neighboring house and toward the view. Redwood louvers at the sides of the balcony let in air and breeze, but effectively hide the other houses.

The main floor is really a self-contained apartment with entry, master bedroom, kitchen and dining area on one level, and steps leading down to the living room and sundeck beyond. As soon as you enter the house you are aware of the view and the whole design seems to draw you towards it. The lower level consists of guest room, study, washroom and a large play area, which is used for summer visitors and can be closed off during winter when the upper floor is heated. Glass doors from the recreation room lead out to a patio.

Structure of the house is wood frame with redwood exterior walls and redwood balcony-screen and trellis. Interiors are kept simple with white-painted plasterboard walls and ceilings, oak floors in the living area and ceramic tile in the bathroom.

Architect: Gina Brandes. *Location:* Sea Cliff, Long Island, New York. *Contractor:* Commercial Construction Corporation.

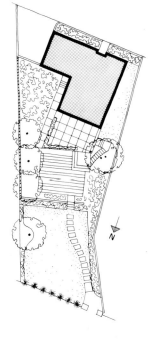

Describing the way in which the scheme developed, Gina Brandes said: "The difference in site elevations caused the house to be one floor high at one street and two floors high at the other. There is a gradual transition from house to patio to garden, following the natural slope of the terrain. The main floor is on the higher level and there are steps—inside the house and out again—following the sloping ground."

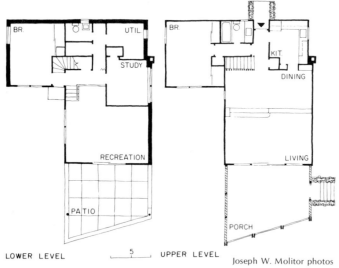

LOWER LEVEL   5   UPPER LEVEL

The open planning of the main floor with its close relationship to the outdoors gives a very spacious feeling to what is really quite a small house. Some nice detailing, such as the redwood screen near the stairs to the lower level, the wood framing between dining and living area, the sitting-steps and storage arrangement in the living room, serve to offset the essentially simple, uncluttered interiors. The dappled shadows thrown by the overhanging trees make sitting on the balcony an unusually pleasant experience.

Joseph W. Molitor photos

The Obata House

Behind the quietly handsome façade of Gyo Obata's own house, five levels dramatically open out onto a beautiful little lake formed of an old quarry site. The house, in fact, is an excellent object lesson for those who feel that contemporary architecture cannot successfully combine the interest of varied interior spaces and levels with the virtues of warm, unaffected simplicity.

The site itself is an unusual one, in the suburbs of St. Louis. It consists of three acres, of which one quarter is an open meadow, one half is wooded area, and the remaining quarter is a lake edged on one side by an outcropping of limestone about 30 feet high. Obata comments that "the main purpose of the design was to create an economical, simple wooden house that would fit into the site so that all the principal rooms would look out over the lake and the rock ledge." Because of the existing slope towards the lake, it was possible to arrange entries to the house from the grounds on two different levels; the lower side being toward the lake to the east, and the main entry from the meadow to the west. Most of the land has been left in the natural state; only the meadow has been seeded for playfields. The slope of the land has also been used to advantage to help shield the open carport under the playdeck off the children's bedrooms.

The western, entrance façade of the house is relatively closed, with the main visual interest given by the pattern of the rough-sawn, vertical board-and-batten redwood exterior. The air of quiet unity is enhanced by window and door framing of dark bronze anodized aluminum, and a roof of dark brown shingles.

The lake façade of the house, however, opens wide to the view with broad sliding glass windows, and is replete with balconies, terraces and porches.

The five levels of the Obata house not only help create strong visual interest in the interiors, but sensibly zone the house.

The "main" level of the house is devoted to the entry and a story-and-a-half-high living room with an ad-

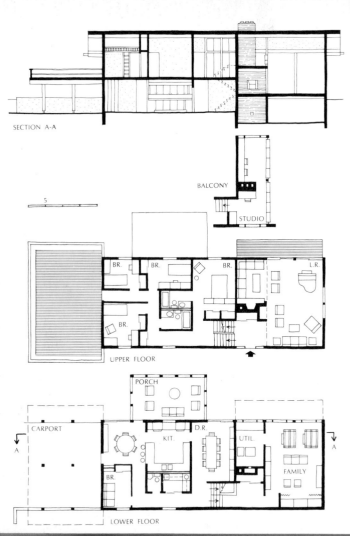

SECTION A-A

5

BALCONY

STUDIO

BR. | BR. | BR. | L.R.

BR.

UPPER FLOOR

PORCH

CARPORT

A

BR. | KIT. | D.R. | UTIL.

FAMILY

A

LOWER FLOOR

joining, low-ceiling inglenook and fireplace. A half-level below these areas is another section containing dining room, kitchen, breakfast area, and a small guest-study area. The carport is also at this level off the kitchen. Down another half-level is the family room and weaving studio. All these rooms face towards the lake. Bedrooms are a half-level up from the entry, and a balcony-studio is above this.

Architect and *owner:* Gyo Obata. *Location:* St. Louis, Missouri. *Engineer:* Al Alper. *Contractor:* E. C. Mikkelsen Construction Company.

Hedrich-Blessing photos

The George House

Small in area, but surprising in its varied spaces, this delightful little house was designed by its architect-owner to make the most of a 90- by 100-foot, extremely steep, eucalyptus-strewn lot.

As can be noted in the illustrations, rooms and levels are disposed in an unorthodox manner to provide all sorts of contrasting big and little rooms, views and shelter—all in 1,500 square feet, and on a very limited budget.

But each nook and window was carefully studied to give the owners the environment they wanted. Malcolm George comments that "it was our intention to set the house among the trees in such a way that it would alter the site as little as possible. By placing the house on the extreme north side of the property, we were able to save all but three of the trees and preserve enough land on the south side for future expansion. As this put our house very close to a house on the north, that wall has been made almost solid for privacy. Another house, to the south, seemed to be a comfortable distance away, and we have provided a deck on that side to catch the afternoon sun. The upper road, and a house across it, are screened by dropping the main level of our house below the road; it became clear that if we were to become really involved with all those trees, the roof had to be opened up—and so the bay window which climbs the roof became our central theme. But well back in the recesses of the house are more protected spaces where we can sit and talk by the fire or sleep tucked under the roof. At the very top is a room in the trees which my wife, who is a teacher, uses for her work." All this adds up to a very successful, "fun" and "big" little house!

Architect and *owner:* F. Malcolm George. *Location:* Berkeley, California; *Engineers:* Forell & Associates. *Contractor:* Eugene W. Monroe.

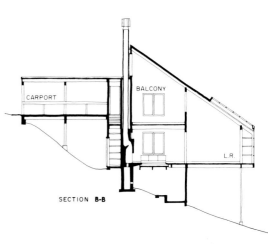

SECTION **B-B**

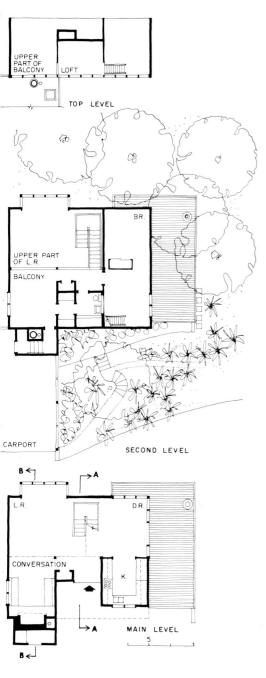

UPPER
PART OF
BALCONY | LOFT

TOP LEVEL

BR.

UPPER PART
OF L.R.

BALCONY

CARPORT

SECOND LEVEL

B ← | ← A

L.R. | D.R.

CONVERSATION | K.

← A

MAIN LEVEL

B ←

5

Warm, natural wood and textured plaster define the interior spaces in a simple but crisply effective manner. The exposed post and beam structure is of rough-sawn fir, with welded steel plate connectors. All ceilings are rough-sawn hemlock, floors are random oak. Cedar shingles are used on both exterior walls and roof, with trim stained a darker color. The underside of the house was left unfilled to "show that it was on a hill" and to minimize foundations.

SECTION A-A

Morley Baer photos

Jerry Duchscherer photos

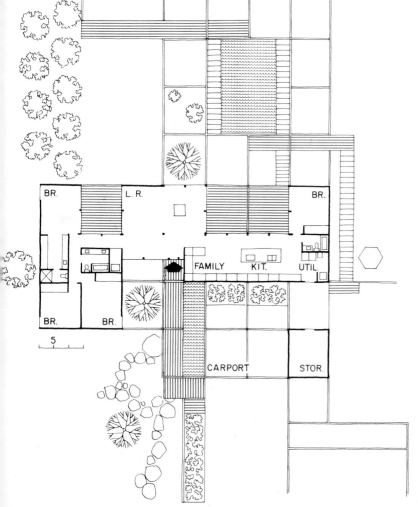

The Beadle House

An asset was made of a difficult site problem in this trim house. The lot was chosen because of its desirable location and its undulating grades. However, it was a natural "wash" which carries off seasonal run-off water from the neighboring hills. To cope with it, the architect simply left the site undisturbed as a natural, pristine rock garden, raised the house on steel stilts, and enjoys the periodic streams running through. The entrance drive and pool terraces were built up

BR.   L. R.   BR.

FAMILY   KIT.   UTIL.

BR.   BR.

5

CARPORT   STOR.

a bit, with block retaining walls, so they would not flood during run-off times. Raising the house itself gave an added bonus in gaining elevation to take advantage of a nice view to the south.

The design of the house contrasts a rather sophisticated, hard-edged structure with the natural rocky environment. It is totally contained in an exposed, modular steel frame with bays measuring 12 feet 4 inches by 14 feet 4 inches. The bays are used open or closed as the plan warranted, for rooms, terraces and planting areas. Enclosing walls are sliding glass doors or panels surfaced with cement plaster. Rooms or terraces were planned to exactly fit a one- or two-bay space. The extensive use of glass walls and integrated outdoor spaces visually enlarges all the living areas in the house. Two combination heating and air-conditioning systems (one three-ton, one five-ton) join with sensible zoning in the plan to provide a very livable house for Mr. and Mrs. Beadle and their five children. In his own house, Alfred Beadle used the regular, disciplined bay spacing as a "design motif" throughout the raised or built-up areas of house and grounds: the same module is used for dimensions of planting beds, drive and the like. In these areas, planting is carefully controlled to contrast with the natural site—a device which considerably reduces the maintenance required for the grounds. It would be possible, if desired at a later date, to enclose some of the open deck areas in the house to enlarge some of the existing spaces, or to add new ones. As built, the house has 2400 square feet of interior space, and 4800 square feet of roofed space.

The steel structure supports wood joists topped by plywood sheathing for floors and roof. The surfacing for the roof is a 4-ply built-up one; carpeting is used on the floors of most living areas. Four-inch batt insulation is installed in floors and ceilings as a thermal barrier.

All the interiors are finished with painted gypsum board, except the big family-room-kitchen, which is surfaced with walnut. All the baths are interior ones, daylighted by domed plastic skylights. All the utilities of the house are ranged along the central bays to form a sort of extended "service spine". In addition to the generous storage provided in each room (including a good-sized dressing room for the master bedroom), there is a commodious storage "house" flanking the garage.

Architect and owner: Alfred N. Beadle of Dailey Associates. Location: Phoenix, Arizona. Contractor: Len Pritchard.

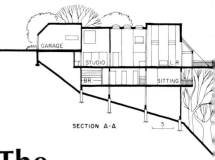

GARAGE
STUDIO   L.R.
BR.   SITTING

SECTION A-A   5

The Friedman House

A steep and picturesque site above the San Francisco Yacht Club on Belvedere Island is the location of architect Rod Friedman's own house. In addition to concern for preserving the stands of oak, eucalyptus and pine on the hillside, he was limited by city ordinance to a two-story scheme. Thus, instead of the compact three- or four-story design one might expect, he has developed a more horizontal concept. Unfortunately, a large volume of enclosed space under the house cannot legally be occupied. Nonetheless, by using an audaciously structured deck and an elegant green-house-like solarium, Friedman has made the most of the situation.

The dining room, living room and library, which occupy the most prominent volume of the house (right) are meant to be places where the family gathers and where parties are held. In addition, each family member has his own private space. For the parents, there is a suite on the lower level which includes a sitting room and smaller deck. The wood-framed house is sheathed in vertical resawn redwood boards left to weather, a contrast to the white interior walls.

Architect and owner: Rodney F. Friedman of Fisher-Friedman Associates. *Location:* Belvedere, California. *Engineers:* L. F. Robinson and Associates (structural); Harding Miller and Associates (foundations). *Contractor:* Clancy Becker.

An adjustable ¾-inch cable each side of the solarium (above) supports the flying deck. From it (above right), one has a remarkable view of the marina activities. From below, the sailors in turn can compare the structure with the rigging of their boats. The lofty living room (right) and the library beyond are filled with light during the day by skylights and large windows on all sides.

The Whisnant House

This house for an architect and his family manifests common sense as well as talent, clear sightedness as well as imagination, practicality as well as dreams. The result is modest, clear and memorable—though it may take some readjustment of our expectations to perceive it, for what we are likely to remember is not an elegant architectural effect here or a striking detail there, or indeed even some dazzling form of the whole. What we will remember is a place made simply of simple materials, well-formed around the needs of the people who live there and attentive to the land on which it is built.

These qualities are not uncommon ideals in house design, and in fact most people would call them downright basic. In practice, though, they can easily get lost in the rush to achieve other more dazzling goals.

WHISNANT RESIDENCE, Charlotte, North Carolina. Architect and owner: *Murray Whisnant*. Engineers: *R. V. Wasdell & Associates* (structural); *J. M. McDowell & Associates* (mechanical); *S. T. Hocsak & Associates* (electrical). Contractor: *G. E. Vinroot Construction Company*.

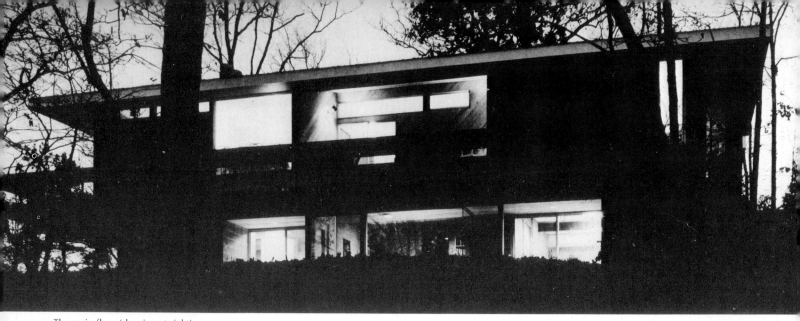

The main floor (drawing at right) is a series of rooms clustered around a central mechanical core that contains the kitchen and two baths. At one end of the plan are three bedrooms and at the other a large living and dining room that opens onto a cantilevered deck (large photo above); in front of the mechanical core is the entrance hall and behind is a small porch reached from either the master bedroom or the kitchen. On the lower level are an office (photo below right), a studio and a playroom.

The configuration of the suburban site and the placement of the buildings next door suggested that the house be relatively closed and viewless on the front and on one end (left photo below); accordingly the living room is lit on the front by a narrow band of windows just above eye level and by a sloping skylight in the ceiling (large photo opposite). At the back of the house (right photo below) the walls open up to provide a view down a wooded hill, both from the back porch and the living and dining room, and from the office below.

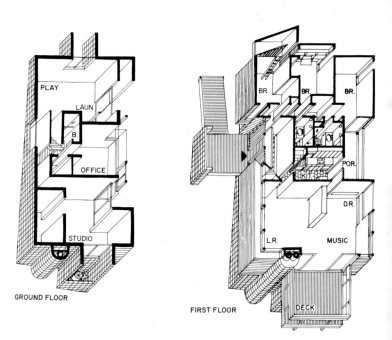

GROUND FLOOR

FIRST FLOOR

Gordon Schenk photos

The Freidin House

An ample, sophisticated house has been achieved on a $30,000 budget (1967) by rigorous but discerning adherence to simplicity in design and materials.

The plan of the house is very straight-forward: a long scheme places studio and guest room at one end of the house for quiet and privacy, family bedrooms at the other end, and living and service areas in the center. A slope in the site is utilized to provide the heater and utility room on a lower level under the west end of the house.

One of the things that gives the house its special character is its precision in the midst of a rambling, wooded setting. Jack Freidin describes its concept as a "house set on a recessed base so that it floats above the ground with controlled views of the surrounding woods. It is clearly separate and distinct from the ground —related to the site, yet not disturbing it. The use of fixed and sliding glass not only frames the view from each interior space, but relates that space with the site both visually and functionally." And one might add that, in spite of the compact, self-contained air of the design, the little recessed, outdoor decks by each of the glass walls provide a very positive and useful link with the grounds from most interior spaces.

The wood frame construction is also kept very simple. Roof joists, 24 feet long, span the width of the house, and are cantilevered, over dropped beams supported on posts every 14 feet. Posts are supported on the exterior foundation wall. The floor framing is the same as the roof, except joists rest on the concrete block foundation wall.

Architect and owner: Jack Freidin. *Location:* Weston, Connecticut. *Engineers:* Wiesenfeld & Leon. *Contractor:* William G. Major Construction Co.

An atmosphere of tidy, unaffected informality pervades the Freidin house. Most surfaces are natural-finish and easy to maintain. The exterior is sheathed with cypress siding. Concrete block used for the foundation is left exposed where the ground slopes to permit a lower level for a utility area.

Some areas of the cypress siding are carried inside as interior finish, but most walls and all ceilings are surfaced with gypsum board. Floors are oak, and have grills for the forced warm air heating.

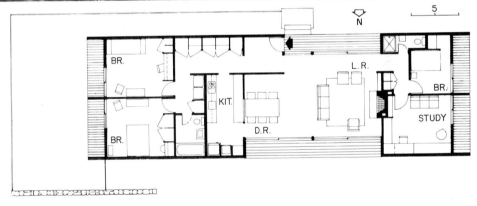

Marc Neuhof photos

The Campbell House

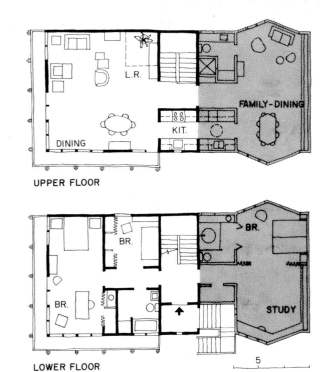

UPPER FLOOR

LOWER FLOOR

5

John Carden Campbell has used a great deal of ingenuity and skill in the design of this very attractive—and pleasantly unselfconscious—house for himself. The greatest problem, as well as the greatest asset, was presented by the lot itself. It is small (60 by 80 feet), steep, uphill and costly ($30,000 in the mid-1960s). But it has a most spectacular water view of San Francisco, many beautiful plum trees, and is in an excellent weather area.

Campbell has outlined his design objectives for a house on this site as follows: "1) to design a very economical house for a very expensive lot, which could be expanded later to justify the original land cost; 2) to make the greatest use of the view; 3) to get two cars and about 1400 square feet of house on the site without cutting the trees; and 4) in addition to these basic factors, it was desired to create a house whose interiors and the exterior were related to each other—to produce an integrated structure on a limited budget."

All these objectives have been handsomely achieved in the final house, which seems unusually spacious for the square footage, and which cost about $27,000 in 1966. In arriving at the three-level scheme, Campbell comments that, "after the cars are on the small lot, one must build over them to save land. For economy, the house is a box sitting on a carport. Also, because of the trees that were to be saved, and to get the most expansive view, the living room, kitchen and future dining room were placed on the top floor. The master bedroom has a good, though not as broad, bay view. And because of the size, the setbacks, the view, and the trees, the house is angled on the site and kept close to the street to leave room for expansion. To integrate the structure with the interiors, specially designed crystal-cut boards were used inside and out for walls, furniture, exterior rails and panels, the front door and even some picture frames."

Architect, interior designer, and owner: John Carden Campbell. Location: Sausalito, California. Engineers: William Gilbert of Gilbert, Forsberg, Diekmann & Smith. Contractor: John Sonne.

Karl H. Riek photos

As the plan (page 29) shows, the Campbell house has been reduced to four rooms by combining functions: a large living-dining room, a compact kitchen, a large master bedroom and study, and a small second bedroom. The scheme permits future expansion to three bedrooms, two baths, dining room and upstairs toilet.

The great feeling of space in the house has been created, not only by using the same specially cut boards inside and out, but by all white interiors, the sense of extension given by the balconies, and the actual shapes and sizes of the rooms. The living room is 21 feet square, with 12-foot ceilings. The idea of unity is further carried out, as can be noted in the photo at left, by treating walls, cabinets and curtains in a consistent manner: The curtains are linen tapers, cut and hemstitched to match the two sizes of the boards, and the same striated pattern is seen inside and out. Yellow, orange and tile red are used as accent colors against the all-white background.

The Zeidler House

J. C. Wilson

In a wooded ravine in the center of metropolitan Toronto, architect E. H. Zeidler has created this remarkably appropriate and livable house for his own family. The site drops about 160 feet vertically into the ravine, which connects with the Don Valley River, and the architect's prime desire was to create a "non-house disappearing into the natural environment of the sloping hillside." As constructed, the house does this extremely well: it is only really visible from one side—the other façades merge with the trees and the retaining walls, to become part of the natural setting. Old stone walls of a previous house were retained in the new structure, which subtly extends and drops with the contour of the land.

A very unusual organization of the plan has been used to zone living activities, and to make the most of the slope of the land, variable daylighting, and the beautiful views the site affords. Rooms are arranged on four levels and divided into a "children section," and an "adult section," linked at the bedroom level and at the kitchen. The kitchen (the second) level is the life center of the house, with dining, family living and work space with a formal entrance to the house on one side, and a children's entrance leading to the pool on the opposite side. From the main entrance, one enters into a dramatic four-story space replete with windows, glass walls and skylight which frame views of the trees, sky and the deep valley below. The adult living spaces—living room, dining room and study—pivot off the core on succeeding levels, each of which has a deck or terrace.

At the top of the hill, only the top-level garage, with a door to the family stair tucked under the overhang, is visible. A "secret room" is behind the garage on this top level, reached by a ladder as a play space for the children, and out of bounds for adults.

Only two basic construction materials have been used in the house: the existing gray stone (relocated in some instances) and rough mill-sawn cedar. The cedar siding is carried over the roof deck surfaces to give an overall design impression of a series of wood decks stepping down the forested hill. They are broken only by the many skylights which illuminate the interiors. Materials inside the house are as restrained as without—all is neutral gray and white, with people, views and art as color accents in the otherwise monochromatic scheme.

Architects: Craig, Zeidler and Strong. *Owner:* Eberhard H. Zeidler. *Location:* Toronto, Ontario. *Structural engineer:* Gordon Dowdell. *Mechanical engineer:* Hardi Craig. *Contractor:* Plorin & Pede.

As in many rooms of the house, the formal dining space (part of the two-story adult living area) is lined with books to double for study and reading. The family dining space is part of the kitchen, family-living and work space; the glass walls lead to an outdoor terrace and pool. The decks and glass bays closely link all areas with the outdoors.

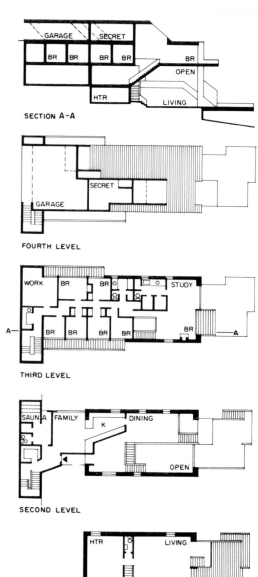

SECTION A-A

FOURTH LEVEL

THIRD LEVEL

SECOND LEVEL

FIRST LEVEL

Panda/Croydon photos

2
Another basic—for almost everyone—is cost. And sometimes the discipline of budget forms the starting point of a house design.

For example, speaking of his house (page 56), architect Henri Gueron explains both a principle and how it was accomplished: "The idea for the house—economy and unpretentiousness—came about out of necessity. I had designed many residences for clients where space and detailing were not a problem. I felt I had always given clients the best of my craft, but could not afford it for our family. With these thoughts in mind, I set up some rigid disciplines to follow:

"I kept all room sizes to an absolute minimum, opening up the otherwise small living area vertically—which does not increase the actual size but greatly increases the visual size. The total square footage turned out to be 985 square feet.

"2. The kitchen was kept to a 7-foot galley type unit. Large custom-designed kitchens are often one of the costliest items in a house.

"3. The plan had to be very efficient to prevent any 'waste' of square footage in circulation space (halls, etc.).

"4. The house was designed on a 4-foot by 8-foot module to take maximum advantage of modular materials such as plywood and drywall—eliminating waste and labor in cutting.

"5. Detailing was kept simple and followed local building practice.

"6. All doors and windows were standard, out-of-the catalog items. One exception: the 6-foot plastic bubble."

This small house, inexpensive but in no way cheap, is perhaps an extreme example of a house where the basic design idea was low cost. It is striking and ingenious—not for everyone, but just right for its owner. And full of ideas for everyone.

Architect Young Woo, whose house is shown on page 58, says: "Staying within a building budget is 'part of the ego trip' for all architects—unless you're one of those fortunate few. How often have I heard the comment: 'Sure, that is a good design . . . considering how much money was spent.' The architect designing for himself wants to prove good design is attainable within a rigid budget, if for no other reason than to prove that he believes in all the design principles he continuously preaches to his client. How successful I was, with my own house, must be judged by someone else. I can say we enjoy every day we are in the house, which I suppose is some measure of a successful design."

Architects designing for themselves have to make the same sort of cost compromises as they would make for a client—there is no magic. Architect Andrew Daland explains that for his own house (page 44) he made "cost cuts I normally would not consider in designing for others. For example, all of the fixed glass was used quarter-inch plate, recycled, as it were, from store-front windows. The floor framing was designed to utilize the maximum efficiency of the members chosen; normally I would overdesign a bit, primarily for psychological reasons, but that was not necessary with myself as a client. I used concrete block rather than poured concrete for the foundation, southern pine rather than oak flooring. Room sizes—especially bedrooms, bathrooms and kitchen—were kept to an absolute minimum; for another client I would be a bit more generous." Despite the cost descipline, Mr. Daland obviously enjoyed building and living in the house: "I encountered no special problems. As a matter of fact, construction of the house was an absolute delight —performed by two men with an occasional helping hand from passersby . . . Although the house was designed primarily as a weekend retreat, I have lived in it continuously for the past year, and it has been a source of great satisfaction to me. It is compact, efficient, and relates closely to its natural surroundings. As a relatively small house, it has been an extremely successful experiment in economy of design, as well as an educational experience particularly applicable to today's market, where building costs are rising at such an alarming rate . . ."

The Riley House

Philip Molten photos

Within the simplest imaginable structural framework of this small (under 1,000 square feet) house, architect J. Alexander Riley has created an extraordinary variety of indoor and outdoor spaces. Essentially, as is best seen in the plan and photo at right, the house is made of two flatroofed units set seven feet apart and bridged by a handsomely framed pitched roof set above twin clerestories that pour light into the center of the house, even though it is on a northeastern slope.

That roof is one of four elements that give distinction and interest to what—in less sensitive hands—could have been quite ordinary. The second design device was staggering the ends of the elements—on both the entry and view ends of the plan—to eliminate any sense of boxiness. Third: dropping the living room floor three steps, and leaving it open to the dining room and kitchen to add a sense of spaciousness. Finally, while the house is of the simplest construction, with posts, single-thickness walls of 2¼- by 6-inch cedar and a single-thickness 2 by 6 cedar roof—great attention was paid to the detailing. Note for example the mitered corners of the clerestory structure (photo right) and the simple-to-fabricate but effective detailing of the interior (photos next page).

Architect and *owner:* J. Alexander Riley. *Location:* Inverness, California. *Contractor:* Jean Madill Burroughs.

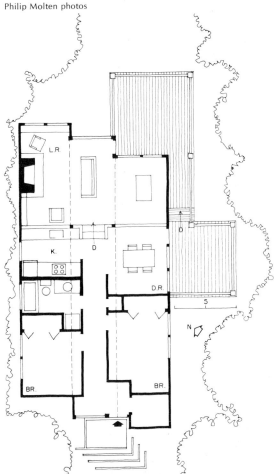

On the interiors, the simple wood framing is clearly expressed, with a small but effective amount of trim and special detailing. The photo (far right) shows the main view wall, with the deck beyond. At right, a view from the living room to the dining room and kitchen three steps above. The kitchen-living room, photo below, emphasizes the changes in scale and room shape worked out within, again, an essentially simple framework.

The Grossman House

A tight budget and an open space program determined the design of this house built by Theodore Grossman for his wife and himself. Twenty-four-foot clear-span wood trusses support the floor and roof, opening up one large living space served by a utility core containing a kitchen, laundry and bathrooms. Core spaces are illuminated by skylights. The kitchen and the bathrooms are the only separate areas.

The house is located among pine trees and small rolling hills just east of the front range of the Rocky Mountains. Interior space is intended to relate to this natural setting and also provide a setting itself for objects and art works which the owners collected while they served as Peace Corps Volunteers in Colombia.

Sliding windows on the long sides are glass infill, permitting expression of the structural piers (all structure is wood); solid end-walls emphasize the direction of the trussed rafters.

Warm colors and materials soften the somewhat severe lines of the house. Siding is light-stained plywood with plank finish (left). Exterior decking is redwood; interior floor in the living space is oak. The front door is bright sky blue. Furnishings emphasize reds, whites, yellows, and black. Total cost in 1970, not including land and a well: $23,400.

Architect and *Owner:* Theodore A. Grossman, Jr., the TAG Associates. *Location:* Parker, Colorado. *Contractor:* Gerle Bros., Inc.

No doors separate the bedrooms and study from the rest of the interior, above. The wall around the study and large closet, right, does not reach the ceiling but serves as a non-structural screen from the living-dining area.

Rush McCoy photos

Phokion Karas photos.

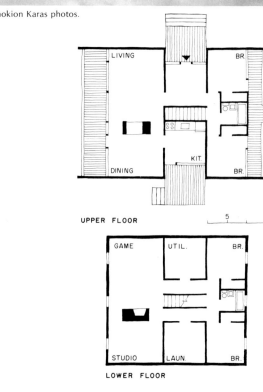

UPPER FLOOR

LIVING · BR. · KIT. · DINING · BR.

5

LOWER FLOOR

GAME · UTIL. · BR. · STUDIO · LAUN. · BR.

The Daland House

This vacation house is good evidence of the continuing use of inventive and playful forms in the design of weekend retreats. Low cost and compact, it uses maintenance-free natural materials. Located on a rugged mountain site and oriented to take advantage of an impressive view to the west, this simple and compact weekend house was designed for both summer and winter use. All openings are deeply carved to form roof overhangs for protection from heavy snow. Steps to elevated decks provide easy access at any snow depth in winter. During the summer, the doors and windows open to the decks and the breeze. Deeply setback porch with cantilevered deck provides additional summer living space, cross ventilation and an impressive view to the west. To create a structure compatible with its rugged site, the architect utilized straight-forward form with strong detailing—shed roof, reverse board and batten siding, and cantilevered decks with heavy railing seats. The house has a compact plan basically divided into a sleeping zone and a living zone, separated by the service core. Two other considerations affected the design: a tight budget ($16,000 in 1967 with unfinished basement and exclusive of furnishings); and minimum maintenance as reflected in the materials used—interior wood ceilings, exterior redwood siding, and use of stains for trim.

Architect and *owner:* Andrew Daland. *Location:* West Bethel, Maine. *Contractor:* Grover & Jordan, Inc.

The Van der Ryn House

This rugged and very original little house grew out of an attempt to provide a specially-designed low-cost vacation home in a beautiful but remote area where building costs are high. It uses prefabricated stressed-skin panels for walls and floors, for an estimated 15 per cent saving over conventional wood frame. In addition to the Record Houses award winner, which was built for sale (right), two even lower-priced versions have been built, shown at left.

The patented structural panels consist of a plywood skin and a rigid, fire-resistant foam plastic core. The core insulates, and the plywood—redwood on the exterior and cedar or fir inside—also forms the finish.

The panels are four feet wide, and the real key to success came in using this module as the basis for efficient plans. The larger house has a 932-square-foot living area. It cost $15,000 in 1968, including a fully-equipped kitchen and bathroom, wall-to-wall indoor-outdoor carpets and electric floor and baseboard unit heating. The second, smaller house to the top left cost $12,000; the third, costing $10,000, was achieved with sleeping alcoves and the use of outdoor decks. Details for all three were designed to scuttle complicated on-site construction steps, and use simple joints and simple finishes from stock materials to help keep costs in line. The larger house took just three days to build, using a four-man crew.

Architect and *owner:* Sim Van der Ryn of Hirshen & Van der Ryn. *Location:* Point Reyes, California. *Contractor:* W. D. McAlvain.

Joshua Freiwald photos

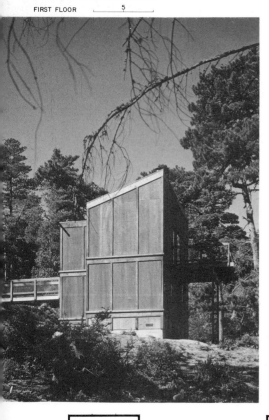

SECOND FLOOR

FIRST FLOOR

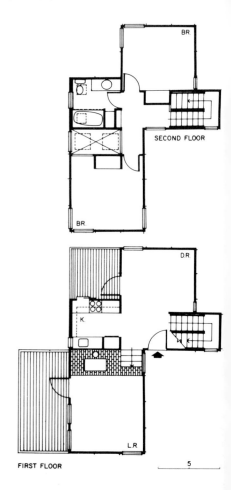

SECOND FLOOR

FIRST FLOOR

FIRST FLOOR

SECOND FLOOR

A number of playful "extras" are built into the two-story, split-level design: The living room with its Franklin stove has a skylit, two-story "well." An overlook from the kitchen can be seen in the photos (below). Wherever possible, outdoor decks are enlisted to increase living space without adding to foundation costs.

47

The Ernest House

An unusual amount of living space for a small, lower cost house was developed in this 1962 house by the architect for his own family. Three major design devices served to gain this goal: 1) a multi-level scheme minimizing roof and foundation area; 2) use of simple, low-cost materials—especially concrete block; 3) the placement of all utilities in a "service tower" to minimize piping, venting, etc.

The end result of these items, plus the placement of the stairs in a second "tower" to balance the service one, has been to free the interior for a number of open living spaces with a wide variety of sizes and views. As added height improved views of the ocean at the back of the site, and also gave better air circulation, major rooms were placed on higher levels, with the lowest floor devoted to stair entry, carport, workshop, and a laundry. The master bedroom, for example, has a clear view of the ocean across the upper portion of the porch.

As the lot is a long and narrow one, the side walls of the house were left blank, with no windows, for privacy from neighbors. The front and rear elevations are kept as open as possible for maximum light, air and view.

Architect and owner: Robert Ernest. *Location:* Atlantic Beach, Florida. *Structural Engineer:* Register & Cummings. *Contractor:* L. L. Abbott.

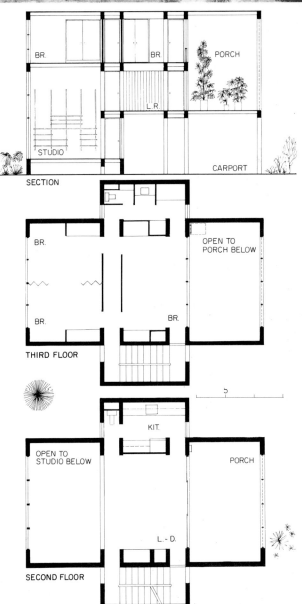

SECTION

THIRD FLOOR

SECOND FLOOR

The structure of the Ernest house is principally of lightweight concrete block bearing walls, with concrete lintels and bond beams; roof and floor framing is wood. The "service towers" flanking the structure also serve as buttresses.

Finishes include clear silicone on the concrete block, gray stain and creosote treatment for wood. With the addition of some stained cypress walls, the interior walls are the same as the outside. Floors are wood covered with ship deck matting in living areas, sheet vinyl in the kitchen, and mosaic tile in the bath areas. All ceilings are wood with exposed beams.

Joseph W. Molitor photos

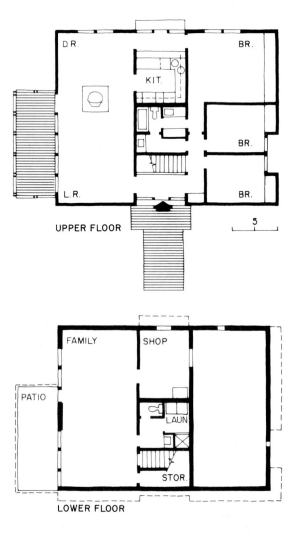

D.R.

KIT.

BR.

BR.

L.R.

BR.

UPPER FLOOR

5

FAMILY

SHOP

PATIO

LAUN

STOR.

LOWER FLOOR

The Glass House

Planned within the limits of a strict budget, this house was designed by the architect as a "first home" for himself, his wife and child—with planned expansion space for later additions to the family. Then (the house was built in 1963) an editor of *Better Homes and Gardens,* Frank Glass needed adequate working space and a pleasant environment for entertaining. The result is a simple, compact two-level dwelling which fits well into the sloping site and uses stock materials to their best advantage.

As the house faces a fairly busy residential street, the front elevation has been left completely closed. Large glass areas on the west and north side of the house provide good light and give a feeling of additional space. The main entrance is separated from the parking area by a wooden bridge.

Frank Glass says that this was done "in order to make the structure 'hang' among the tree limbs."

Although the total floor area of the house is only 1,500 square feet, clear-cut zoning gives considerable privacy to individual members of the family. Stairs connect the children's bedrooms on the upper level directly to the family room below and the play area outside. The kitchen, stair, bathroom and hall separate the entertaining area from the bedrooms. The well-placed entrance foyer, unusual in a house of this size, frees the living areas of general circulation. The cantilevered screened balcony on the west side of the house is shaded by overhanging trees, making a pleasant extension to the living room.

Architect and owner: Frank R. Glass. *Location:* Des Moines, Iowa. *Contractor:* Fritz Gookin.

The Des Moines house is of post and beam construction on a concrete block foundation. Basement walls are of concrete block, painted where they are exposed. Plywood or glass panels in standard sizes were used for the rest of the exterior walls. Describing the exterior of the house, Frank Glass says: "The contrast of textures and the planned, rather formal balance of the exterior was achieved with stock materials. These materials, which required little cutting, were applied with careful detailing in pleasing proportions to give the house order." Exposed insulating deck is used for ceilings and floors and provides a base for the tar and gravel built-up roof. The photographs show how, inside the house, the dark posts supporting the ceiling beams form an effective contrast to the light-colored gypsum board wall panels.

The dining area is separated from the living room by a prefabricated fireplace, which rotates on its base to serve either end of the over-all room. A breakfast bar in the kitchen saves space and provides a convenient base for serving food to the dining room. The house is heated by a forced air system.

Hedrich-Blessing photos

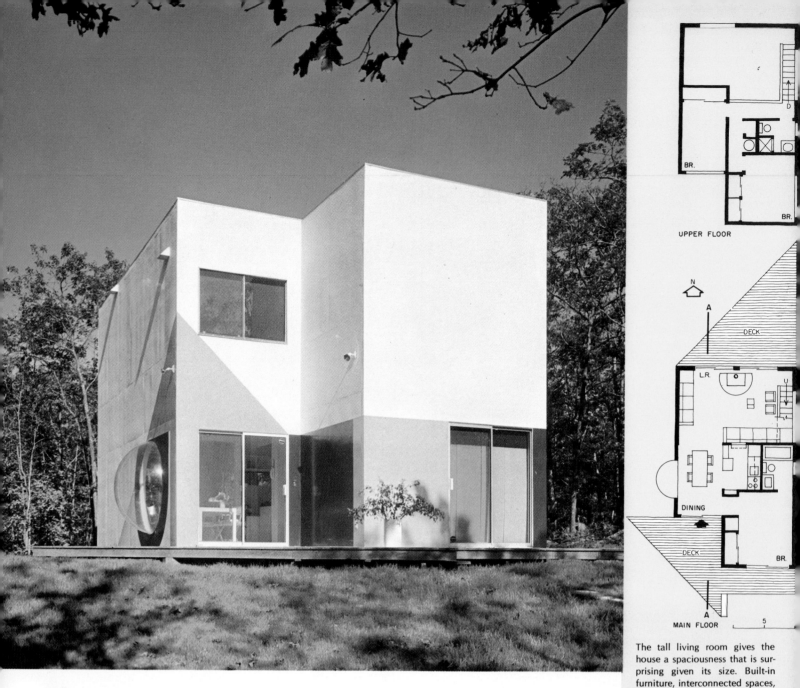

UPPER FLOOR

MAIN FLOOR

The tall living room gives the house a spaciousness that is surprising given its size. Built-in furniture, interconnected spaces, and large windows looking into the woods in three directions also help expand the space. The section reveals a tiny, secluded roof deck reached by a ladder.

Ben Schnall photos

The Gueron House

In 1971, architect Henri Gueron built himself this three-bedroom house (including equipment, insulated, and finished interiors, as well as site work) for $15,000.

Gueron lists four ways by which he accomplished this feat: 1. Square footage was kept as low as possible, barely more than the zoning minimum of 975 square feet; 2. The house was designed on a 4- by 8-foot module, horizontally and vertically, since standard-size plywood was the ideal material for his design—both economically and esthetically; 3. Almost all prefabricated elements are also standard (the principal exception is the acrylic dome in the dining area which cost $110); 4. He served as his own general contractor for an estimated saving of 20 per cent and detailed the house to be easy to build. He

estimates that done for a client using standard contract procedures, the cost would have been about $25,000.

The crisp exterior is ⅜-in. resin-impregnated plywood applied to the studs. The caulking is a white elasto-meric sealant. Two coats of latex acrylic semi-gloss paint were used both on the exterior and on the dry-wall interiors. Finally, the bright accent colors of epoxy enamel were added. Placed diagonally on a long narrow lot studded with the scrub oak typical of eastern Long Island, the house is invisible from the road in summer but during the gray winter provides a brilliant flash of color for passers-by.

Architect and owner: Henri Gueron of Gueron and Lepp. Location: East Hampton, New York. Engineer: Ken Smith (electrical).

56

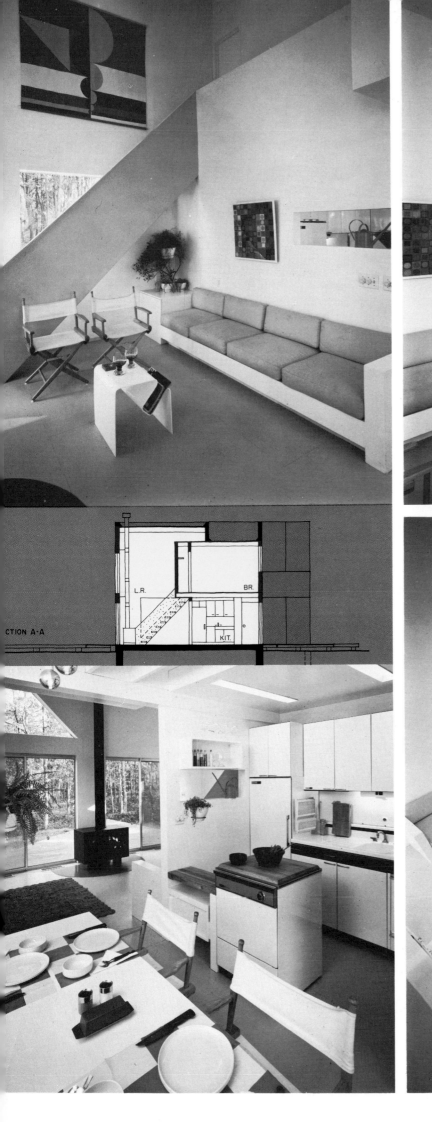

CTION A-A

L.R.

BR.

KIT.

A dramatic entrance stairwell—where fast growing trees and plants create an interior garden effect—is an ingenious solution to the problem of a steeply sloping site. At the same time, the stairwell provides an interesting focus for the main living areas. The device of a raised roof with a band of clerestory glass over the stairwell and dining area is skillfully employed to bring extra light and space into the center of a relatively small house. A handsome stand of eucalyptus trees flank one side of the site which can be glimpsed through these clerestory windows.

Of simple wood frame construction, this house—designed by the architect for himself and his family—makes substantial use of redwood for exterior and some interior walls and for the trellis (above left) which screens exposed glass areas from the sun and also gives shade to an outdoor deck.

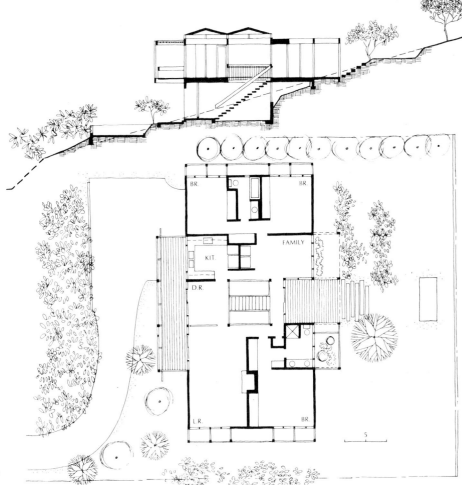

The Woo House

Some well-grown groups of trees on the southern and western sides of the lot protect the house from the heat of the late afternoon sun. An expansive view of the Los Angeles skyline is fully exploited by glass walls in the living-room, dining room and kitchen. A patio and terraced slopes at the rear of the lot make a pleasant playground for the two children, who can be easily supervised from the family room which overlooks this area.

Careful zoning allows plenty of living and entertaining space for the adults without conflicting with the children's activities. The children's bedrooms at one end of the house are separated by the kitchen and family room from the main living areas.

A carport and turning area have been cut into the hillside below the house and a steeply sloping driveway leads down to the street. The construction cost, exclusive of landscaping, was about $26,000 in 1966.

Architect and *owner:* Young Woo.
Location: Los Angeles, California.
Structural engineer: Tom Woodward.
Contractors: Colletta & Edgley.

Leland Lee photos

61

The Holmes House

Architect Dwight Holmes' house on Tampa Bay seems very much at home in what he calls "a near perfect example of semi-tropical environment: moderate temperatures, bright sun, generous rainfall and daily breezes off the Bay and Gulf." Placed well back from the street on a long and narrow lot, the house looks east across the open bay. Largely solid side walls of unfinished concrete block screen the house from uncertain future development on adjoining properties. The end elevations, however, are completely transparent. Four-panel sliding aluminum window walls stacked three high (left) form those façades. To control sun and to provide protection from tropical storms, a system of adjustable redwood louvers has been provided. The louvers have a shadow texture whose scale is adequately proportioned to the masonry planes. Within the severe rectangular volume, Holmes has created an appropriate openness by placing the dining and master bedroom platforms on the second and third floors at opposite ends of the plan, permitting two-story spaces for both living and dining rooms. The central utility core is designed to minimize interruptions of ventilation flow. Including central air conditioning for periods of intense heat and humidity, the house and a small studio behind it of similar construction cost $28,000.

Architect and owner: Dwight E. Holmes. *Location:* Tampa, Florida. *Contractor:* Ranon and Jimenez.

Wade Swicord photos

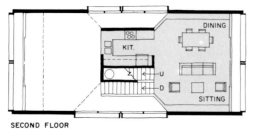

THIRD FLOOR

SECOND FLOOR

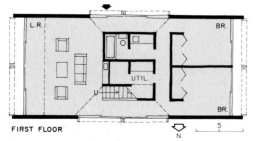

FIRST FLOOR

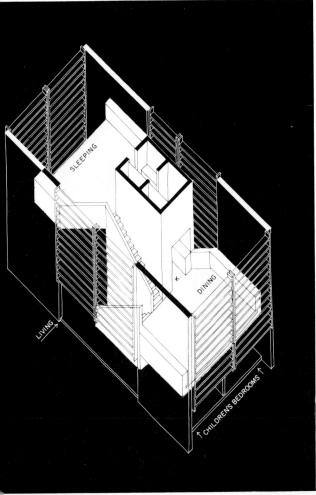

Alternating platforms above the ground floor (section left) create two-story spaces in the living room (below) and the dining room (above) The interior kitchen, open at both ends (right), is well-ventilated and has a good view of activities in the living room as well as outside on the terrace and the adjacent beach.

3

Whatever else is the starting point for design, the needs of the family are paramount.

And meeting the simple physical requirements—enough bedrooms, for example —is the easiest part; what is harder is meeting the subtler needs of the members of the family. "To build a house is something very special. It is a magic circle you draw around the life of a family or a person," says architect Eberhard Zeidler, whose house is shown on page 32. "That magic circle is then filled with life and you feel its power when you enter it."

Writes architect Edward Killingsworth about the wishes and needs of his family that shaped his house (page 66): "We wanted a house with large rooms and spaces which gathered together so that there was great breathing space; and the house is that way. With 3,300 square feet in the house, there are relatively few rooms—so all are large.

"We wanted high ceilings and a lot of glass, again for breathing space. The house is that way. All ceilings are 12 feet high and the house is mostly 12-foot sheets of glass.

"We wanted absolute privacy. So our glass house is set in gardens surrounded with 12-foot high walls.

"We wanted (and here is a very special

requirement) a house that would accommodate a theater or symphony orchestra in the garden, with all the amenities of a fine theater. We have that in the garden, where we can seat 200 with a pavilion portion of the house set apart as a stage. My oldest son used the house for seven years for his Virginia Country Theater, and during this period over 2000 people a summer enjoyed the house and the garden theater.

"We wanted a house which could accommodate large parties comfortably. The house does this, with its large rooms and high ceilings and gracious gardens. One hundred people are comfortable in the spaces."

Mr. Killingsworth expresses the feeling that people who truly enjoy their houses experience: "This house has grace, warmth, and a delicate quality which has been the basis for my other work. Architecture can be a frustrating and difficult business, and I often arrive home exhausted. But when I enter the beautiful free space of this house, life is good again. The house, over our years of living in it, seems to improve each day and seems to respond to our love for it."

The Killingsworth House

A walled compound of pavilion-like rooms, each with its outdoor counterpart, gives an unusual sense of space and luxury to this house. And the dominant theme of intermingled gardens and rooms is all-pervasive: even the central core of the house is a sky-lighted "garden room," and baths have little private patios for sunbathing. An extra spatial dimension was also given to the house by using 12-foot-high ceilings and doors.

Killingsworth comments that his planning problem was "to develop a residence for a family of four, with a minimum number of rooms of maximum size to accommodate large groups of friends or clients." A special provision was convertible garden space for outdoor concerts and theater, with seats for 200.

A very big interior space was created by using an open plan for entry, living, dining and family room areas. As the kitchen is also an extension of this space, and only partially screened by baffle walls, all the cabinets were "designed as furniture". For the boys' bedroom, which is the size of two normal rooms, a "suite" was created with sliding dividers, which separate the room into two sleeping areas with a sitting area between. The master bedroom is enlarged by a large, relatively open, dressing-bath area, which has a "two-story" closet to take advantage of the 12-foot ceiling height. At the opposite end of the house are two more isolated rooms, which serve as a study-design area for Mr. Killingsworth and as an office, lounge and hi-fi area for the theater group. The house has 3,200 square feet.

Architect and owner: Edward A. Killingsworth of Killingsworth, Brady and Associates. *Location:* Long Beach, Calif. *Contractors:* Stromberg and Son. *Interior designer:* Stan Young of Frank Bros.

Julius Shulman photos

THEATER

L.R.

KIT.

FAMILY

OFF.

ST

BR.

STUDY

BR.

BR.

GARAGE
UNDER

10

N

The entrance to the Killingsworth house is through 12-foot-high doors, into an enclosed garden with a long shallow reflecting pool. A pergola-like structure projects into the garden, and doubles as outdoor living area and a stage for music and theater. Portable plywood panels are used to convert the open pavilion into a proscenium-type stage.

The exterior walls of all the main rooms of the house are glazed floor-to-ceiling to closely link the garden areas with the indoor spaces. Even though all living areas in the Killingsworth house are conceived as a big, open plan, some sense of separation is lent by the use of alcoves, colonnades, and differences in floor treatment. Some areas are carpeted, while the central family room, kitchen and service areas have the same brick paving as outdoor terraces and walks. Hot water radiant heating is installed in the concrete floor slabs. Walls are wood frame and plaster.

The Sorey House

Seclusion and privacy are effectively combined with an expanded sense of space, created by open-plan, glassed-in living areas in this strong and forthright house. Although natural woods and heavy foliage help screen the site from surrounding suburban houses during the warm months, architect-owner Thomas Sorey, Jr., has carefully integrated story-high stone walls into the design to assure privacy to both indoor and outdoor living spaces. To contrast with all the openness below, the upper, bedroom floor is securely closed-in on the long sides by shingled exterior walls; this unbroken space is banked inside with a plethora of storage closets. All bedrooms have windows at the ends of the house, while the central (largely service) areas are skylighted.

The plan is well arranged for the family of parents and two small boys, and is devised to permit some changes in future years. For the present, the young children have an entrance via the utility room, where they can shed dirty or wet clothing and wash without tracking through the house; they also have access to the kitchen dining space without having to go through the major rooms when the parents are entertaining friends. The boys' bedrooms are primarily study-sleeping areas adjoining a skylighted playroom.

For later years, the boys' rooms have been built with non-load-bearing partitions which can be totally rearranged as needed. The master bedroom at the other end of the floor is quite large, and doubles as a sitting room; rough plumbing is provided in one of the closets for a future kitchenette so the children may "take over" the downstairs for parties when they are older.

Architect and *owner:* Thomas L. Sorey, Jr. *Location:* Oklahoma City. *Engineers:* Sorey Hill Binnicker. *Landscape architect:* William Warren Edwards. *Contractor:* Keith Hickox.

The crisp, clear-cut character of this contemporary house with its series of intersecting and interlocking planes, acquires a comfortable, near-traditional feeling by the use of familiar materials. In fact, from certain angles, the slight batter of the shingled walls of the upper floor give a strong recall of a mansard roof. Natural, golden brown colors pervade all the materials used gray-beige stone, light brown shingles, and darker brown-stained trim. The windows are also in keeping, with redwood sash and bronze screens. Similar colors and textures are inside: ochre-colored concrete floors, stained cedar walls, and white plasterboard ceilings. The approximate cost of the house itself was $54,600.

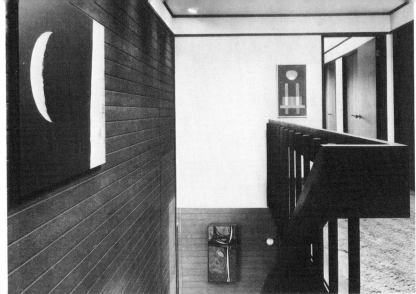

Tom Sorey, Sr., photos

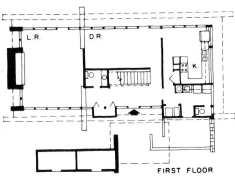

FIRST FLOOR   SECOND FLOOR

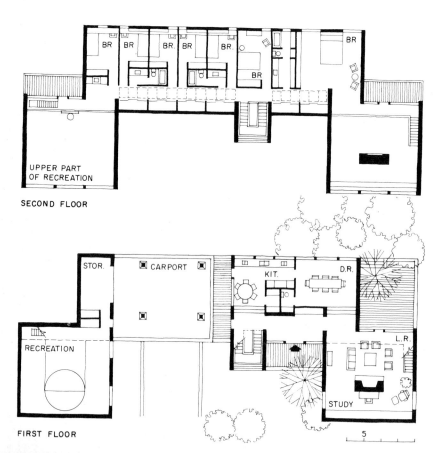

SECOND FLOOR

UPPER PART OF RECREATION

BR BR BR BR BR BR BR

FIRST FLOOR

STOR. CARPORT KIT. D.R.

RECREATION L.R.

STUDY

5

This Lexington, Kentucky home is the reflection of a philosophical attitude of architect-owner Hugh Bennett toward his own family: Parents and children are equals, at least in so far as the spaces designed for them are concerned. The Bennetts have five, and the democratic decision to give each—and guests as well—equally sunny, airy and spacious bedrooms has resulted in the grouping of these along the central, second floor hall. The living room, moreover, a great, two-story space creating a major element at one end, is exactly duplicated in floor area and height by the children's playroom, which serves as the second major element, flanking the bedroom corridor on the other side. The playroom gets direct access to the bluegrass field for outdoor play. A breezeway on the first floor and the stair tower flanking it are both placed to assure the relative privacy of children's and parent's wings. But permissiveness obtains only to a point: the scheme assures that children's activities can be overseen. And there is plenty of opportunity for the family to be together as well. The relaxed, informal approach pervading design of the house is evident in its setting and its strong relationship to the outdoors. The house is built on one of several subdivisions of an 88-acre farm. "There were not that many trees around, since it was all once a horse farm," explains the architect. "We chose the parcel with lots of trees."

Architect and *owner:* Hugh H. Bennett of Bennett & Tune. *Location:* Lexington, Kentucky. *Mechanical engineer:* Bruce Kunkel & Associates. *Landscape architect:* Horst Schach. *Interior design:* Bennett & Tune. *Contractor:* Pope-Cawood Lumber & Supply Co., Inc.

William Roughen photos

The Bennett House

The basic material—used effectively both inside and out—is an economically available "reject brick". Framing lumber is used for all trim and detail, and no finished wood is used. The brick is load-bearing, supplemented by wood frame. Upper floor clerestoried bedroom hall becomes a bridge serving as a conection between playroom and living room. Living areas have walnut floors. Exterior is poplar beveled siding (carried also through upper bedroom hall for non-scuff surface) and esposed brick. The cost of the large house, including gas-fired forced-air system, was $53,000.

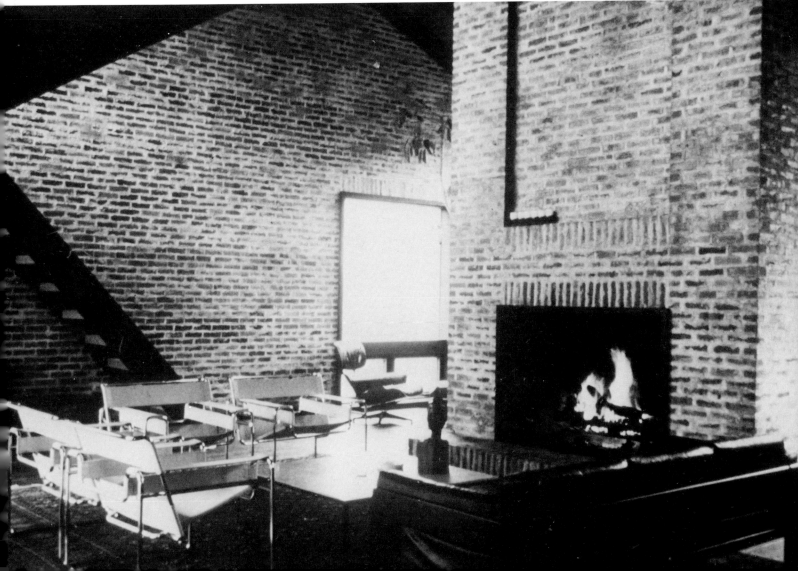

John Oldenkamp photos

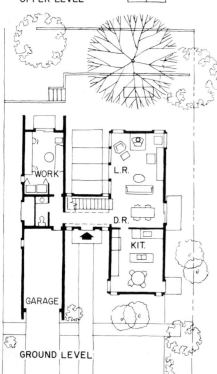

UPPER LEVEL

N

5

GROUND LEVEL

GARAGE

WORK

L.R.

D.R.

KIT.

BR.

OPEN

BR.

BR.

OPEN

The McKim House

Economy and privacy were two important design criteria for architect Paul McKim's own townhouse. Built on a small, narrow lot, flanked on both sides by neighboring houses, the residence affords the McKims a good deal of privacy, and a nice sense of the outdoors.

For a house containing 1,600 square feet of living space, the construction cost of $21,000 is low, especially when the beautifully detailed results are considered. Costs were kept to the budget by using a wood-frame, post-and-beam construction with large plaster panels on both the interior and exterior surfaces.

Basically, the design consists of two rectangular wings linked by a stairwell (see plan at left). The two courtyards, formed between the wings, give the desired outdoor space and privacy.

The house is zoned so that the children use the left wing and the parents the right. This means of zoning seems to be a good answer to maintaining a level of privacy suitable to both parents and children. The children's bedrooms were placed over the "work" area, which could double as a play room in bad weather.

The interior is enlivened by opening up of the one-story space in the dining area to two-story spaces on both sides—in the living room, and in part of the kitchen.

An especially nice attention to details is evident in this house. Everything—from the trellis which spans the front courtyard and casts strong shadows down the white plaster wall (see photo right), to the hooded balcony over the garage—achieves the greatest effect by the simplest means. Even the white walls of the courtyard serve the secondary purpose of reflecting the sun into the north side of the living room.

Architect and owner: Paul W. McKim. *Location:* San Diego, Calif. *Landscape architect:* Wimmer & Yamada. *Interior designer:* Dixon Morrow Jr. *Contractor:* John Worobec.

An extremely important factor in this architect's own townhouse was the low budget of $21,000. Despite such a small budget, he has achieved striking spaces—including the big two-story living room and a variety of outdoor areas as well.

4

For some contemporary architects, a "response to tradition" is the starting point.

The urge for a sense of tradition runs strong in all of us, of course. But a limited view of tradition is responsible for the proliferation of fake Colonial houses that so mindlessly sprawl across the country. Shutters and a cupola do not make a Colonial house. And all tradition is not New England Colonial. The houses in this collection explore tradition—or better, regional architecture—in more sophisticated and far more rewarding ways. For example:

Explaining his house in rural McLean, Virginia (page 90), architect Avery Faulkner says: "One of the design challenges we assigned ourselves was to see whether it was possible to design a house that was both contemporary and respectful of the historic architecture of the region. I had been reminded by a lecture of Paul Rudolph [one of America's boldly innovative and experimental architects] that regional architecture is gradually disappearing in this country. My wife and I took a long trip through Virginia with notebooks and cameras and saw all the great mansions and manor houses we could find. Since the house was to be built in Virginia, it seemed to us that it would be interesting to attempt to find in a contemporary vocabulary those things which would link our house with the houses of the past. High ceilings, the biaxially symmetrical plan, the use of red brick with white trim (in this case, precast concrete) seemed to have much to do with the things that made the James River Plantations significant. The fact that this house was subsequently published as one of five or six contemporary buildings in a new book on the history of Virginia architecture, published by the Richmond museum, encourages me to think that we succeeded in holding hands with the past without compromising my own interest in contemporary design."

Another design experiment that perhaps seems far removed from tradition, but in fact is closely related to traditional forms, is architect John Desmond's house (page 86). "The idea for the house developed after my wife and I saw a Japanese tea house and its surrounding garden. There seemed to be a special relationship between this open pavilion and the garden which completely surrounded it. This became the basis for the central section, or living room, of our house—which is much different from the typical room having only one open exposure. The living room, then, expresses the basic concept of space lightly outlined by steel, covered by a roof plane, open on all sides to the garden. Other areas of the house are similar; except that solid wall areas are used as needed to give the required amount of privacy. However, the non-load-bearing quality of the enclosing brick planes is made clear by the glass strip between their seven-foot height and the roof plane above.

"While this house gave me freedom to experiment, there were no special problems encountered. The local steel works and glass company cooperated in the fabrication of the steel frames and the specially designed mullions, and in the mitered glass corners designed to minimize the enclosing glass planes. After 12 years, I still believe this is the best space I have ever built . . ."

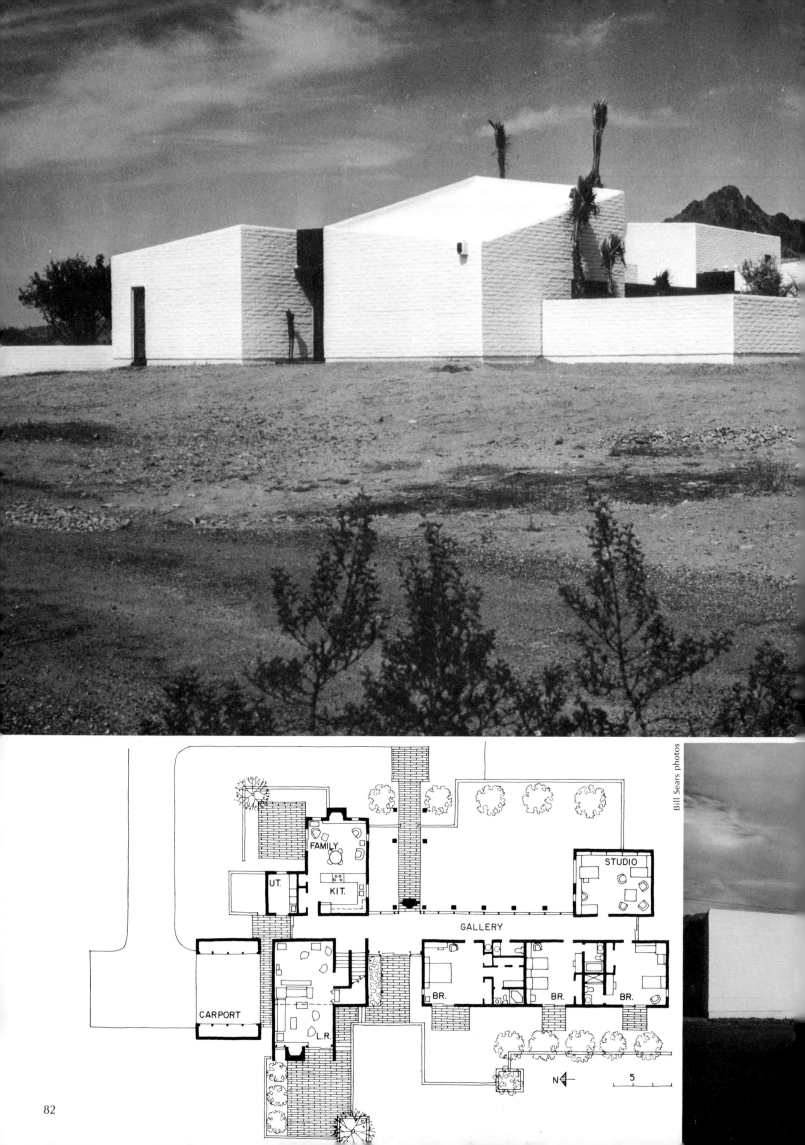

FAMILY

UT.

KIT.

STUDIO

GALLERY

CARPORT

L.R.

BR.

BR.

BR.

N

5

The Gonzales House

At first glance, this is a very regional Arizona house; but much more important is its expression of the universality and adaptability of some of the current contemporary-design idioms. Shed roofs, a relatively loose (but well-zoned) room arrangement, variety in ceiling heights and levels, a "tumbled" (but carefully studied) interplay of exterior forms, and experimentation with light, shade, shadows and views, are all design devices which are being employed in many of the newer houses from Maine to California. Of course, most of these concepts—the shed roof in particular —are just as indigenous to the Southwest as to New England. The singularly local quality that they project in this house stems mainly from the use of adobe-like, mortar-washed concrete block (instead of the wood plank, cedar shingles or brick of other regions), and the desert flora.

It is a quite sophisticated, contemporary house, with privacy and space well organized for a family of four. And, over-all, the design has considerable sensitivity and verve—with one small lapse at the entrance, where some columns and panel doors salvaged from several razed buildings have been added, and which are rather out of scale and character with the freshness of the design. It is certainly one of the more interesting of the newer houses in Arizona.

In planning the house for his own family, Bennie Gonzales comments that, "materials and the form of construction were chosen for their suitability to the climatic and cultural aspects of the region. Set in virgin desert, and buffered with a series of 'green' patios, the house is oriented inwardly, yet opened to the west for the extraordinary desert sunset."

Architect and owner: Bennie M. Gonzales. *Location:* Phoenix, Arizona. *Engineer:* William Meier. *Consultant:* Richard Joachim. *Contractor:* Frank Gonzales.

A variety of pleasant, comfortable spaces are provided throughout the house. And it fulfills Gonzales' own program quite well: "Because this residence had to provide privacy for both small and large groups, the rooms are isolated so that various activities need not interfere with each other. The separate portions of the house are clustered as if independent units of a self-sufficient nature. The more or less public areas are comprised of the two-level living area (with a dining mezzanine serviced by a dumb waiter); a study which can serve for conferences with architectural clients; and a generous gallery, which serves both as hallway and as a spacious area for large numbers of guests in 'party conversation' or at small tables for luncheon. Guests seemingly have access to the whole house, yet younger members of the family can retire to their own quarters. The bedrooms are self-contained, and have sliding glass doors offering a generous view of the desert over an expanse of green. The kitchen is a sort of keeping room, and is spacious enough for leisurely breakfast or lunch."

The Desmond House

This unusual house advances a kind of planning seldom carried out to such a degree in this country. Each major activity area is housed in its own separate "house." All are linked by corridors and gardened areas.

It is a concept that has been highly developed through the ages in various sections of the Orient. And of course, there are slight echoes of Southern Colonial planning, which often had detached kitchens and "garçonierres." The compound houses of the Orient, in particular, have intrigued architects and public alike for some time now, and perhaps this concept is of more fundamental value than some of the stylistic surface treatments we have seen. It is not a big house, but seems vast. Glass walls and sliding doors permit full use of the grounds most of the year. Privacy is assured by a brick screening wall at the front, a bamboo thicket around the lot, and draperies for each pavilion. Use of a simple, repetitive structural scheme kept the cost moderate.

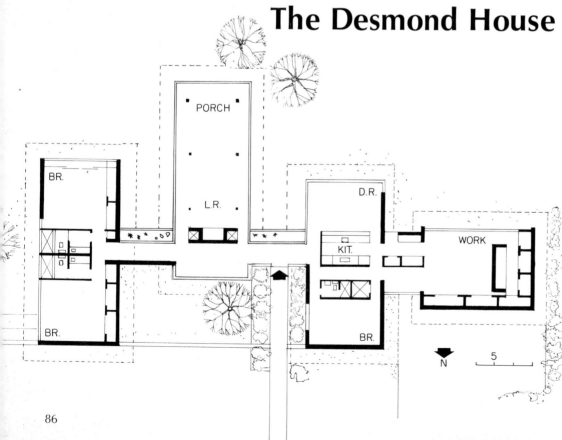

PORCH

BR.

L.R.

BR.

D.R.

KIT.

WORK

BR.

N

5

The site measures 140 by 150 ft, and has a large number of pine trees and some oaks. The property will eventually be completely screened with bamboo.

The plan of the Desmond house was designed for a family of four, parents and two boys. The study is a multi-use room, serving for the architect's professional work at night, and also for a guest room when needed. The room has a hide-a-way sleeping mezzanine over the bath and storage area for guests' children. The area labeled Work Room is located near the kitchen, as it mainly accommodates the avocations of the lady of the house, as well as indoor play space for the children.

The structures of the various units of the house are independent, with light roof canopies held free of the walls by light steel rigid frames using 4-in. WF sections. These are exposed throughout and placed to suggest a definition between seating, dining, or other areas. These units are connected by 7-ft-high hallways with flat roofs, which emphasize the pitched roofed units; and give a welcome change of scale inside. Foundations are concrete; exterior walls are 10-in. brick cavity wall or glass. Interior walls are brick or plywood, high ceilings are acoustical plaster, and low ceilings are wood. The sash is aluminum awning type; sliding doors have steel frames.

Central heating units and hot water heaters are located over the dressing areas and bathrooms, and a heating unit adjoins the fireplace stack.

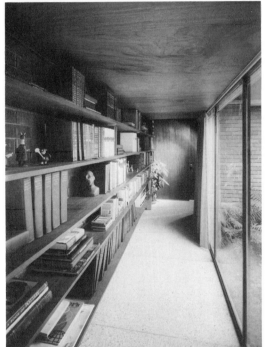

Architect and owner: John Desmond. *Location:* Hammond, Louisiana. *Contractors:* Ragusa Brothers.

Frank Lotz Miller photos

The Faulkner House

The historical traditions of Virginia as reflected in its regional architecture had a considerable influence on the design of this house. Before embarking on this design for his own house, the architect and his wife took a long trip through the state and were particularly impressed by the James River plantations and by Williamsburg. Avery Faulkner says he felt that it was very important to "recall some of the architectural history of Virginia in an era when regional character seems to be disappearing."

The symmetry of the plan, the rather formal elevation, the use of soft red brick with grape-vine joint, and the feeling of height in the two-story entry hall and living room all recall the elegance of the colonial period. But the low, rectangular silhouette of the house, and the meticulous handling of window details demonstrate clearly that the architect's in-terpretation of traditional themes had a strongly Miesian background. Despite its admitted debt to tradition, the house has much character of its own and demonstrates Faulkner's individual approach to architecture. The precast concrete cornice—intended "to give the house a strong visual cap against the sky"—the full-height concrete frames around all door and window openings, and the placing of the glass area in the center of the front elevation reveal a highly personal expression of traditional and contemporary themes.

Architect and owner: Avery C. Faulkner. *Location:* McLean, Virginia. *Structural engineers:* James Cutts— Gongwer & Kraas. *Mechanical engineers:* Frank J. Sullivan Associates. *Contractors:* Davis, Wick, Rosengarten Co., Inc. *Landscape architect:* Lester Collins. *Interior designer:* Ethel Pilson Warren.

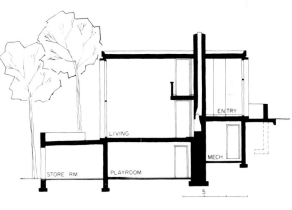

STORE RM   PLAYROOM   LIVING   ENTRY   MECH

5

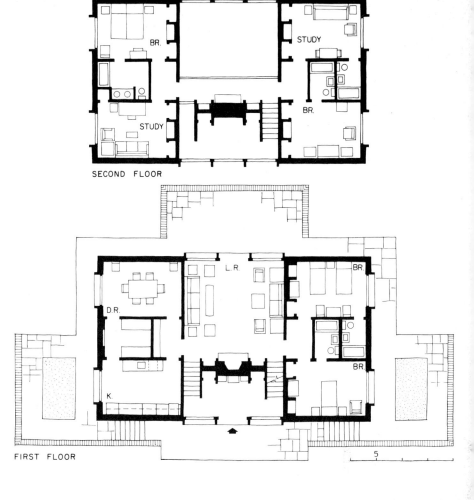

SECOND FLOOR

The Faulkner house is sited on a steeply sloping wooded lot overlooking the Potomac river, which is a quarter of a mile wide as it passes the house. The building sits on a bluff some 175 feet above a waterfall. Landscaping is intended to supplement—with azaleas, dogwood, hollies and laurel—the natural oaks and poplars.

The plan of the house is symmetrical and relatively formal, and is organized around the two-story living room, which opens to a terrace and the river. The high-ceilinged entry hall, placed halfway between first and second floors, is connected by stairs to the living room, which is flanked on one side by the dining-kitchen area and on the other by a guest bedroom. On the second floor, the master bedroom and study on one side are connected to the children's wing by a balcony over the upper part of the living room. From the balcony it is possible to see across the living room and terrace and down to the waterfall beyond.

FIRST FLOOR

5

PARKING

Norman McGrath photos

The Partridge House

In designing and building for his own family, architect Lawrence Partridge had no original intention of buying an existing building to remodel as a home, but an old New England barn with its beautiful glacial stone foundation and walls had a compelling appeal. Together with program and site, the scale and character of the parts of the 1890 structure which were saved established the scale and character of the design.

The stepped slope of the site suggested the roof relationships of the three new sections which were added to the existing structure (the rest of the barn was demolished). Thus, the fragmented appearance of the house was in part planned to reduce the scale of these walls. The various wings contain—from the left of the photo—dining room; kitchen and a bedroom; stairhall; and, in the old building, family room on the lower level, with two bedrooms and bath located on the second floor and a workroom office on the third. An arrangement of fixed insulating glass window, bi-folding storage cabinet, wood door ventilator and screen was designed for use throughout the house, further contributing to the strong exterior rhythm and scale. Roughsawn fir shiplap siding painted white and a white cedar shingle roof respect a New England vernacular and offset the original walls. Contrasting interior materials include natural wool carpeting for living areas, natural red oak trim and drywall, painted white, except where glacial stone walls are left exposed.

Architect and owner: Lawrence Partridge. *Location:* Weston, Massachusetts. *Engineers:* Arthur Choo (structural); Terenzio Genovesi (heating and ventilation). *Contractor:* Costa Limberakis.

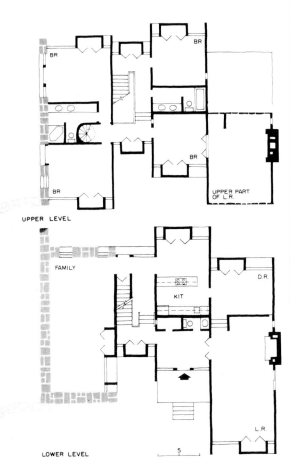

UPPER LEVEL

FAMILY

KIT

D.R.

L.R.

LOWER LEVEL

5

The living room reaches a dramatic 23-foot height. The photo (right) is taken from an upper-bedroom opening designed to provide added ventilation for the living and dining rooms. Below is the master bedroom whose curved windows are openings of the original wall.

5

Sometimes a planning idea —a special arrangement of rooms to suit a particular family— forms the starting point for design.

For example, architect Alfred De Vido explains his house (shown on page 110): "The house was intended as a weekend and summer house, with studio space to permit work on the weekend. The house was also intended to serve as a design laboratory for a number of experiments, both spatial and technical. In the house, we clustered small bedroom areas around a large central room. The theory was that large bedrooms were not required in a vacation house, and it was more important to have a large interesting social area. This has worked satisfactorily, although the master and guest bedrooms could be larger.

"We thought we wanted an open kitchen —this is frequently requested in vacation or weekend homes. But it has certain practical disadvantages and we have since partially enclosed it.

"The extra-wide casements and sliding barn doors are excellent for summer use, since they permit 100 per cent opening of the void. For the winter, the casements worked out well, but the barn doors proved somewhat drafty and required additional weatherstripping.

"The small elevated studios work well

for private use, but are unsatisfactory for conference use. Their spatial relationship to the rest of the house is, however, quite pleasant."

Architect Rodney Friedman explains the
planning of his larger house (page 20): "Because this is a family home designed
for individuals who enjoy their privacy as well as companionship, the plan is
purposely compartmented so that the family members may enjoy one another's
company by choice rather than necessity. All of the rooms on the upper level
are designed so that they may be used as family meeting places as well as for
social functions. A painting and drafting studio is located between the garage
and kitchen. On the lower level there are the individual children's rooms and
the master bedroom suite, which includes a sitting and study area approximately
18 feet square—and this space enables the adults to entertain simultaneously
or retreat in comfort at the times the children are using the first level for social activities. The house was completed and we moved in during the summer
of 1971, and we are all extremely happy with it. It is intended to be our per-
manent home."

The Seidler House

Concrete, because of its ability to span long distances, is the material architect Harry Seidler chose for his own house. Because of the rugged site's beauty, the architect wanted to preserve it intact. Therefore, the house took on a primarily vertical dimension in order to follow the contour of the steep hill. The garage was placed at the top of the hill to avoid landscaping for a driveway.

After leaving cars above, the approach is down steps and across a suspended entrance bridge into the top one of the four levels of the house.

In the center of the house is an open two-and-one-half-story space from which all levels begin. The plan is a simple rectangular one but is divided into a sunny northern part for daytime activities, and a shady southern part for quiet, passive uses, separated by half-flights of steps.

Architect and owner: Harry Seidler. *Location:* Killara, Australia. *Engineers:* P. O. Miller, Milstone & Ferris; *lighting:* Edison Price. *Landscaping:* Bruce Mackenzie. *Contractor:* Peter Cussel.

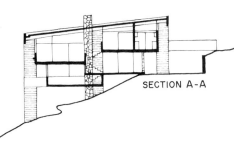

SECTION A-A

STUDIO

A

FAMILY

A

UTIL.

BR.

BR.

BR.

BR.

LOWER LEVELS

10

L.R.

D.R.

K.

BR.

STUDY

UPPER LEVELS

The photo, left, shows a glimpse of a through view from the living room level which gives a sense of the areas beyond without blunt openness of planning. The structural piers, the fireplace, and the concrete parapets define these through spaces.

All levels open onto ample covered outdoor living areas and suspended terraces. These create good shading and assure coolness in the hot summer months.

The five-bedroom house is constructed of rough-sawn board-formed concrete and other maintenance-free masonry. Three rows of reinforced concrete piers support suspended and cantilevered floors—stiffened by rail-height parapets that make the long projections possible.

Floors in all living areas are of quartzite stone; only the bedrooms and the library-study are carpeted. The main sloping ceiling is Tasmanian oak boarding.

Max Dupain photos

The Morgan House

Opposing triangular volumes butt against each other to create the strong massing in architect William Morgan's year-round house for his own family on Jacksonville, Florida's Atlantic Beach. Stepping down the flank of a primary dune, on an ecologically fragile site, the house opens at every level toward the ocean but maintains its privacy with blind walls at the sides and rear.

The entry level contains living and dining spaces, kitchen and garage. Parents' bedroom and work area are on the mezzanine above, and bunkrooms for the Morgans' two teenage sons are set on the level below. A central stair, linking all the levels, introduces a powerful diagonal around which the principal spaces of the house take shape.

The simple geometry of the forms is carefully matched to the profile of the dune and is reinforced by the bleached wood siding laid up in a pattern of opposing diagonals. A system of concrete grade beams and slabs, built over pilings, supports the wood frame. The skill with which the Morgan house is fitted to its site accounts for a good deal of its success. But just as important is the clarity with which the architect has developed his ideas and made them hold up, without noticeable compromise, through construction and final finishing.

When first published as a project, the house drew criticism from several correspondents who felt the site had been treated without sufficient regard for its ecological sensitivity. Some said the site should not have been built on at all. Such questions may still fairly be raised, but the continued stability of the dune, the return of the dune grasses and other plant and animal life are all encouraging.

MORGAN RESIDENCE, Atlantic Beach, Florida. *Architect and owner:* William Morgan, *Structural engineers:* Haley W. Keister Associates, Inc. *Lighting consultants:* William Lam Associates. *Contractor:* Ross Construction Company.

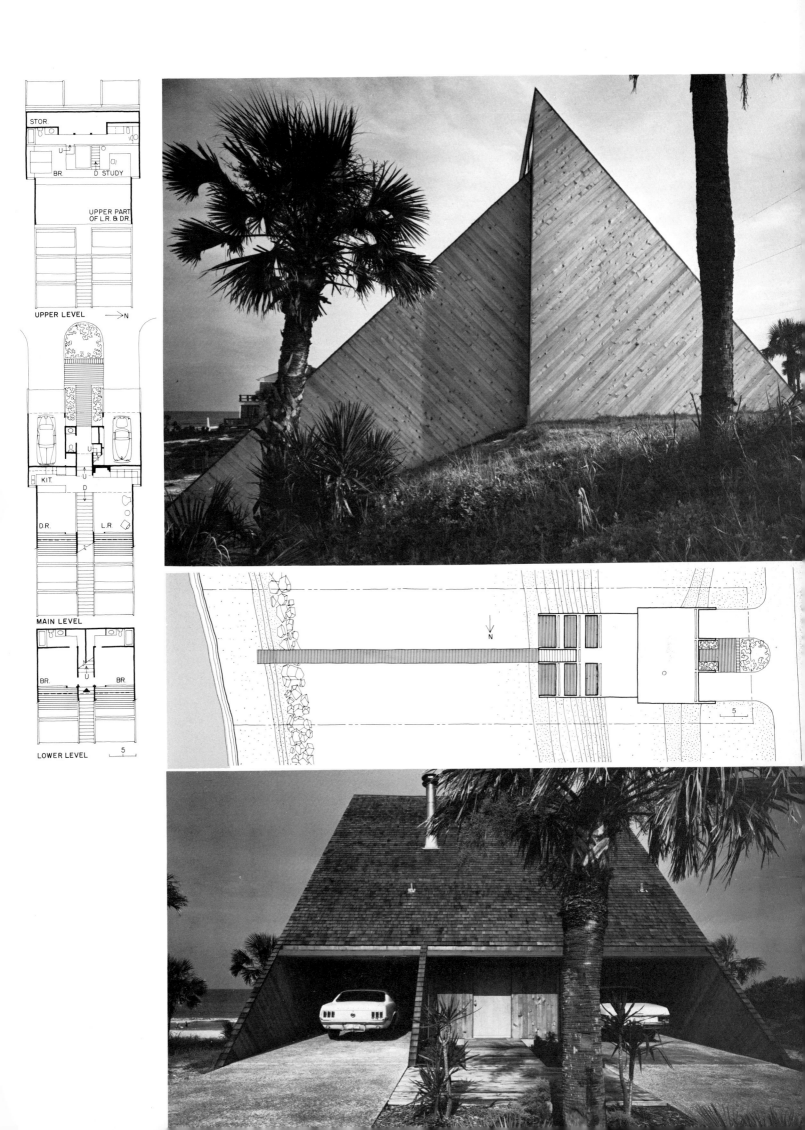

STOR.

BR.   D STUDY

UPPER PART
OF L.R. & D.R.

UPPER LEVEL   N

KIT.

D.R.   L.R.

MAIN LEVEL

BR.   BR.

LOWER LEVEL   5

N

5

Daylight penetrates deep into the interiors. The main spaces are indirectly backlighted from high clerestory (see section perspective, at right). The outer sidewalls are washed with light from vertical strip windows at the juncture of the two triangular volumes. Together, these various sources generate a pleasant level of natural light throughout the house.

Tom Yee photos (courtesy of House & Garden)

Ronald Thomas photos

The Lovett House

The site: Crane Island in Puget Sound's San Juan Island Group. The architect and owner: Wendell Lovett. His program: a small, low-maintenance vacation retreat for his own family that would provide a complete change from urban routine.

The resulting structure is only 12 feet wide and contains just 370 square feet of enclosed space including a small sleeping loft reached from inside by a simple ladder-stair. Inverted bow-string trusses support the roof and suspend the deck that cantilevers 18 feet over the foundations. Within this structure, Lovett has fitted a compact kitchen, plumbing essentials, minimum storage and space for sitting and sleeping six. All furniture is built-in. The level of the deck drops one step (the depth of the joists) inside to accommodate the mattress seating.

Much of the fun of this house comes from the boldness of the concept: the tightness of the plan contrasted against the audacity of the long cantilever, as well as from the skill with which the house exploits the site and view. The detailing is neat and clean throughout but never fussy, and retains a very pleasant sense of informality.

In form and color, the interiors carry through the design theme stated so simply and forcefully on the exteriors. There is no wasted motion in the design and hardly a space or element that is not put to multiple use. Of all the houses in this collection, perhaps none is conceived and executed with more singleness of purpose or realizes its design goals more completely.

All structural lumber is Douglas fir. Exterior and interior cladding is rough sawn cedar stained to match the bark of surrounding trees. Cost of construction was approximately $15,000. A beautiful site; a challenging program; a neat and imaginative solution.

LOVETT VACATION HOUSE, Crane Island, Washington. *Architect:* Wendell Lovett. *Structural engineer:* Robert Albrecht. *Contractor:* Wendell Lovett *with* Clifford I. Hooper.

Christian Stub photos

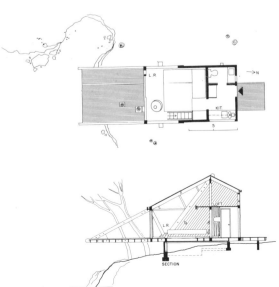

SECTION

The DeVido House

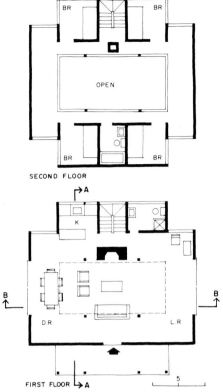

SECOND FLOOR

FIRST FLOOR

This sophisticated little vacation house epitomizes the reaction of city dwellers against the small, standardized rooms of today's apartments, and their strong desire for big, soaring spaces in their second homes in the country. As architect De Vido puts it, "I wanted a large living space—shaped, textured and dramatic—to contrast with the more mundane shapes of apartment living."

He has achieved this in a striking manner, and within an extremely reasonable budget—about $21,000 for the house alone in 1968. The heart of the concept is a big, three-story space, filled with sunlight. At the lower, living levels, this space extends to the outdoors through two sliding glass walls. Four bedrooms, small but adequate, and two fair-sized lounge/bunk areas are on the second or balcony level. At the very top are two aeries, reached by retractable ladders, for work and drafting. Big banks of windows on two sides provide light and views for these platform areas. These spaces, plus two baths and a small, open kitchen, provide most facilities of a very big house.

The house is situated on a long and narrow strip of woodland, and was designed to provide privacy on the two exposures closest to the neighboring lots and views of the woods and flowering shrubs on the other sides. The house is boldly symmetrical, with

the main approach on the center axis, via a covered entrance porch and a path from a parking area.

The design itself is a discerning, rustic understatement, with exposed structural parts and natural wood finishes used throughout. Variation and accent are achieved by texture— cedar shingle outside, rough-sawn cedar walls and polished white pine floors inside—and by a darker stain for the trim. The total effect is one of ease and warmth and freshness.

Architect and *owner:* Alfred De Vido.
Location: East Hampton, New York.
Contractor: Pete De Castro.

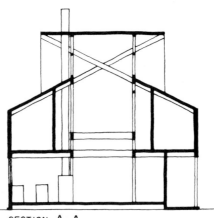

SECTION A-A

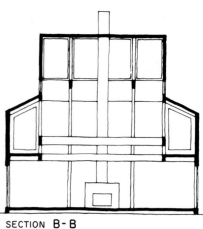

SECTION B-B

The structure consists of a basic Douglas fir post-and-girt system (on a 5-foot module), plus four central columns and "x" trusses to support the highest roof. The exterior wall is insulated, and all glass is insulating, to allow electric heat in winter.

© Ezra Stoller (ESTO) pho

The Rex House

On an upland meadow south of Yosemite, architect John Rex and his family planned a house that serves as the nucleus of a working cattle ranch. The house rests gently on a carpet of wildflowers, and is built around an entry court landscaped in stone, gravel and tufted greenery. If the court is stylistically mannered, it is also conceived and executed with loving attention to detail. The specimen boulders, pitted and covered with lichen, were assembled from various locations around the ranch and placed with evident care. Blocks of bedrooms on the south side of the court are linked to each other and the rest of the house by covered walks that are closed in winter and used as hothouses. In summer, these corridors are thrown open to a prevailing westerly that is funneled through the court to the covered terrace.

The living room, zoned informally for small and large groupings, opens to the north and southeast to frame wide-angle views of mountain and meadow. The whole scheme is visually unified by a continuous flat roof that keeps the silhouette low and contrasts with the distant Sierras.

Principal materials are slump stone and resawn cedar inside and out. Floors are finished in custom tiles colored to match the surrounding soil.

Architects: Honnold and Rex. *Location:* North Forks, California. *Owner:* John Rex. *Engineer:* Greve & O'Rourke. *Landscape architect:* Edward Huntsman-Trout. *Interior design:* Guy Moore and Associates. *Contractor:* F. D. Wilcox.

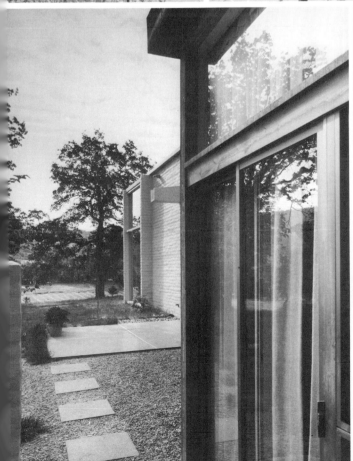

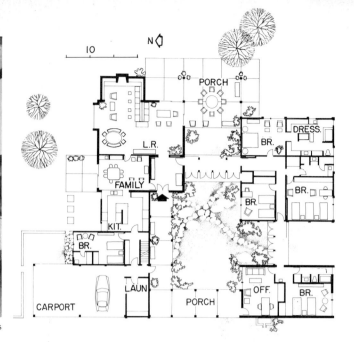

Leland Lee photos

Living room subdivides easily to accommodate groups of various sizes. A small alcove with its fireplace provides an intimate setting for winter evenings. Ceiling height is raised to 16 feet over the rest of the room and furnishes entertainment space at a grander scale. Couches are covered in cowhide and all accent colors are chosen to match local wildflowers that bloom in profusion each spring.

In the kitchen (below) which opens into the family room, meals can be prepared for as many as one hundred guests. Photo (above) shows corridor buttoned up for winter. Bedroom (right) has its own entrance and opens generously to a view of country once inhabited by Mono Indians.

The Schlesinger House

A very different scheme has been developed to gain privacy in this Pennsylvania house. The site is a small, exposed corner lot in a typical residential neighborhood. The architect decided to build a two-story house that turned in on itself rather than look out toward non-existent views.

To accomplish this, the smaller utilitarian spaces required in the house (baths, kitchen, stairs, utility room, fireplace) were pulled out to the building's perimeter where they are enclosed by load-bearing masonry walls. The solidity of these walls screen the larger, open living spaces, which are organized around a two-story, top-lighted dining space at the center of the house. In effect, the house

has a "core" of space rather than of utilities. View windows are provided at the ends of the house.

The plan uses a slope in the site to gain an entry at half-level. The lower floor is given over to children's areas and more active family activities, including kitchen and dining. The upper floor is principally the domain of the parents and includes living room, studio, master bedroom. The "well" permits some supervision of the lower level.

Architect and owner: Frank Schlesinger. *Location:* Doylestown, Pennsylvania. *Contractor:* Doylestown Building Co. *Landscape Architect:* Jeanne Schlesinger.

Marc Neuhof photos

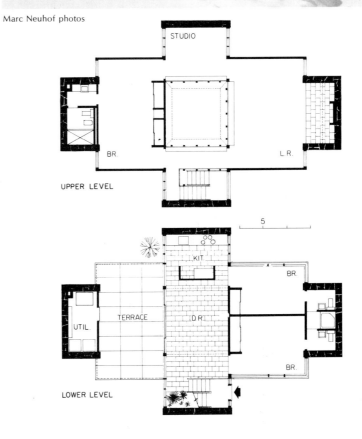

STUDIO

BR.

L.R.

UPPER LEVEL

5

KIT

BR.

UTIL.

TERRACE

D.R.

BR.

LOWER LEVEL

119

Although very open, with spaces flowing together, the plan segregates activities, and provides a good degree of privacy. The windows and terrace on the lower level are masked from the street by a hedge. As noted previously, all utility or service areas are housed in stone "pylons," which are finished with a silicone waterproofing and are exposed inside and out. The stone forms bearing walls. The rest of the structure is of wood frame, with cedar clapboards on the exterior. Interior partitions are wood stud, surfaced with clapboards or plaster. Ceilings are plaster, except in the kitchen, where fir is used. The roof is built-up. Floors on the upper level are birch; on the lower level, they are slate and vinyl asbestos tile. Sash throughout is aluminum. Heating is by a radiant panel system, in the floor slab of the lower level, in the ceiling upstairs. The terrace has floor heat and glass walls for winter use.

The Alcorn House

UPPER FLOOR

LOWER FLOOR

Some fairly unorthodox techniques, both in planning and over-all design, were used by James Alcorn of Skidmore, Owings & Merrill in this house for his family in Berkeley, California. As he describes it, the house is "situated on a 45-foot-wide lot which slopes up from the street at the rate of 2:1, and commands a cloistered view of the Berkeley campus, the Bay Bridge, and San Francisco beyond. Due to the steepness of the site and a desire for a usable outdoor area, it was deemed feasible to locate the living room and adult area on a lower level, thereby placing the kitchen, dining room, laundry and children's area above and adjacent to a sheltered outdoor deck.

"The main views from the house are located in a diagonal relation to the front face of the house, and by canting the supporting walls in the line of view a larger viewing area was obtained.

"The design of the house grew, as it were, by a study of subtraction. From a cube, notches and openings were carved to provide the desired views and penetrations. A vertical penetration of the second floor and roof culminates in an 8- by 8-foot skylight, which has fixtures for night lighting from above. This central space and adjacent gallery is the hub of daily activity."

The house has a balloon frame, on concrete piers, grade beams and retaining walls. The exterior is surfaced with natural cedar shingles, and has aluminum window frames and black trim. The roof is tar and gravel. Interiors are finished with white-painted gypsum board. Ceilings in the living areas are Douglas fir. There are approximately 1950 square feet of floor space.

Architect and owner: James Leigh Alcorn. *Location:* Berkeley, California. *Contractor:* Kenneth Feenstra.

Some extremely interesting interior spaces have been created in this modest-sized house by using platforms, balconies and a central light well. Outdoor play and living space has been provided on the steep site by a deck-terrace opening off the top floor of the house, as can be seen in the section. The kitchen is also on this level for easy outdoor service.

Karl H. Reik photos

The Kiaulenas House

Vassia and Laura Kiaulenas, a mother and daughter who are both architects, have devoted more than ten years of their own labor to complete this project. The result is a residence whose ordered, rigorous architectural concept has been realized with a richness of detail that no one building by conventional means could afford today.

The house was designed as a suitable place to hang the collection of paintings by her husband, Petras Kiaulenas, who died in 1955. His large handsome representational paintings in strong frames are hung everywhere about the house. They sometimes seem at odds with the openness of the house which is anything but a museum. It is a dilemma not unlike that posed by the Guggenheim Museum. Here, too, the vigorous Wrightian idiom, responding as it does to the dynamics of nature, overpowers the static canvasses hung there. It is that tension, however, that gives the house its exceptional vitality. The site was part of an abandoned overgrown estate. In 1959 the design was complete and ready to build. Bids on the erection of the 12 main beams that make up the structure were much higher than expected—$7,000 to $8,000. It was the connections between beams which bothered potential erectors; after Mrs. Kiaulenas took two days to detail the cuts required for each joint, the price dropped to below $1,200, and she was able to proceed. The contractor, Gustav Poerschke, was a great admirer of Frank Lloyd Wright and attacked the job with pleasure. He built the masonry tower and raised the beams but then died. There was no other contractor to be found and it was then in 1962, at her daughter's suggestion, that the two began to build it themselves,

coming out from New York City on weekends to pursue the work.

The next two years were the crucial ones for the whole project. While Mrs. Kiaulenas and her daughter, who was beginning her architectural studies at Cooper Union, were enclosing the structure with roofing and the skylight and windows with temporary sheets of building board, the community was responding with petitions to have the house demolished and continuing acts of vandalism.

At the same time, a developer proposed to subdivide the estate surrounding the knoll on which the house stands. Mrs. Kiaulenas responded by preparing for the Town Board a comprehensive plan covering an area of 25 square miles (a three-year volunteer effort) that proposed recreational uses for the nearby land since it contained attractive lakes and hills which neighboring colleges could use. The plan was accepted virtually unaltered after a series of political confrontations. The only major alteration to the plan was that the land immediately next to her property was allowed to be used for a housing subdivision. The two women continued their weekend labors. Stairs, plumbing, cabinet work, panelling all were completed over the next six years.

"But no moment gave me such delirious joy," says Mrs. Kiaulenas, "as the day I hung the paintings. As far as I can remember it was the first day that I sat doing nothing. Nothing but looking at the paintings and the trees through the windows and skylight and the plants under the paintings. Every bad memory was swept away."

Architects and owners: Vassia and Laura Kiaulenas. *Location:* Staten Island, New York

126

W. A. Boetcher photos

Based on a trapezoidal plan, the structure consists of a two-piece ridge beam which bears at its upper end on a masonry tower. Four smaller beams frame the large acrylic skylight over the kitchen and dining room. Except for the masonry and the 12 beams that make up the basic structure, the two women did all the work themselves. All parts of the house are open to nature: the lower rooms through the skylight and the upper ones through glazed walls which have views of Long Island Sound over the roofs of the recently-built development houses. A small swimming pool nestles at the base of the tower, protected by a delicate curving fence of lumber atop a retaining wall. The paintings, plants and rich carpets complement the carefully-detailed interior of the house. Most of the surfaces, unfinished redwood, are articulated with small repetitive elements cut from stock lumber using bevels and kerfs in a Wrightian manner. Flooring and ceiling patterns echo the triangular plan of the house. The kitchen has parquet counters and panelled doors of alternating beveled squares of sapwood and heartwood. Two huge fireplaces, almost large enough to walk into, dominate the upper rooms. At the entry, a mirrored wall turns the tiny plant-filled space into a bright and welcoming introduction to the dramatic volumes above.

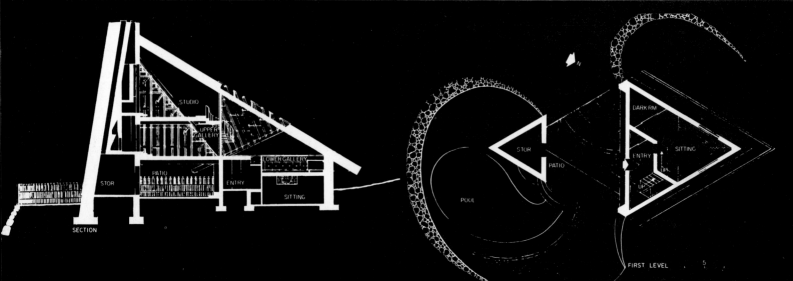

SECTION

FIRST LEVEL

5

UPPER GALLERY   LOWER GALLERY

BATH

UP   UP

UP

SECOND LEVEL

STUDIO   DN

DN

THIRD LEVEL

6
Many architects—in their own houses—experiment with forms and plans and structures they would not ask a client to risk. And this is one way house design evolves.

One example is architect Tasso Katselas' house (page 148): "The house was approached with the idea of solving the intricate and myriad problems of family life . . . However, it was also approached with the idea of experimentation. The use of standard concrete forms to accomplish a series of spaces that vary one from the other simply by changing direction was tried, and proved to be economical. Empirical cantilevers were tried. One of the special problems was that form work for these delicate cantilevers had to be removed by me—the workmen were hesitant to take responsibility for the sagging they were certain would occur. None did."

A far cry (perhaps the farthest cry) from experimenting with structure is this experiment by architect Hobart Wagener: "Our house (page 140) began with our love for plants and trees and flowers. One must work hard at gardening in Boulder [Colorado] since the days are hot and dry in the summer, cold and very windy in the winter. We reasoned that with the wonderful Colorado sunshine all year, we could enjoy a garden inside the house, under a skylight, and spend the least amount of time to obtain maximum 'growing' results protected from the difficult natural elements. Our concept was that the space for the garden be large in scale to accommodate massive, dense growth; and that most other areas of the house would depend upon this garden for privacy and visual interest.

"The plants and trees have grown rapidly and are constantly a source of pleasure and changing color. Bougainvillea is one of the more successful vines, with intense color in its blossoms. Our banyan tree and Australian tree fern each have about seven-inch trunks and fill much of the garden. We have already sawn down several trees that reached the 26-foot-high skylight.

"Special problems are related to the greenhouse-like conditions. Tremendous heat build-up from the skylight in the summertime was anticipated, and the air-conditioning system has proved to be adequate. But since the trees and plants have grown large, they give off so much moisture that excessive humidity became a problem, which we are attacking with an exhaust fan. Architecture provides no solution to aphids in the garden, so we are now trying ladybugs." ·

Perhaps the most experimental of the experiments is the house of architect Richard Foster (page 132). His house, at the touch of a switch, revolves, on the bearing of a warship gun turret. The site that justifies such gymnastics is a superb one—it has a long-distance view to a reservoir, a short distance view, and a view up and down a slope; points of interest for over 270 degrees. Says Mr. Foster: "This design was not an attempt to do something spectacular. It was simply a continuation of the thought given every project I am involved in. The problem was simply to design a house exploiting the qualities of the site to a maximum. It was, in fact, the fifth design for the site. We have lived in the house for nearly five years, and find it even easier to live with and more enjoyable that could have been anticipated. It is difficult for those who have not sampled the possibility of reorienting their home on a whim, to imagine watching the sunset from the living room, turning 180 degrees to watch the moonrise, then turning another 90 degrees to see the play of night-lighting on the pine forest."

The Foster House

The unusual glass-walled revolving house shown on these pages was designed by architect Richard Foster for his own family on a six-acre site in rural Connecticut. Rejecting many more conventional schemes, the architect arrived at the final design as the ultimate response to the site's breathtaking, near-perfect view of the surrounding countryside. For fullest advantage of the view—farmland hills and a distant lake to the west, a meadow and nearby pond to the east, and a pine forest to the north —the architect enclosed his circular house in glass, set it on a pedestal, and made it rotate for changing landscape, sun and mood.

The circular house is anchored to its site by a concrete pedestal which contains entry, staircase and various utilities, and supports a 14-foot-wide ball-bearing ring which in turn carries the entire superstructure. A control panel regulates motion which varies to five feet per minute and is barely perceptible. The house is very special, but it is also a year-round, everyday house designed for an active family. The architect's solution successfully achieves complex organization for living while preserving the unity and symmetry of a self-contained formal shape. For all the ingenuity of plan and mechanical detail, the real interest and delight of this beautifully detailed "machine for living" lies in the high degree of refinement with which the radical architectural design has been conceived and carried out.

Natural-finished materials are unexpectedly appropriate to the circular house: beautifully-weathering pre-rusted steel; cedar shingle cladding for curved soffits; glazed, hexagonal-shaped tiles for unusual floor shapes.

Spaces within and around the house received as much attention as the view from it. The approach—through a walled motor court, beneath the great tree-like superstructure to the pedestal entry—offers a varied spatial sequence while gradually revealing the breath-taking view.

Architect and owner: Richard Foster. *Location:* Wilton, Connecticut. *Engineers:* Zoldos and Meagher *(structural);* Meyer, Strong & Jones *(mechanical). Landscape and interiors:* Richard Foster. *Contractor:* William Mewing.

Ezra Stoller (© ESTO) photos

Floor and wind loads, which with the 30-foot cantilevers could not be carried to the ball bearing supports by beam action alone, are in fact hung from a series of tension-ring-bound vertical trusses. Asymmetrical loads are redistributed by both the roof-top tension ring and a second, horizontal truss network and then transmitted down by hall columns to a massive reinforced concrete ring, which rests on the bearing points. The sheer weight of this 50,000 pound ring further stabilizes the rotating superstructure. The central column is nonstructural, serving rather to carry pipes and wiring from core to rotating connections.

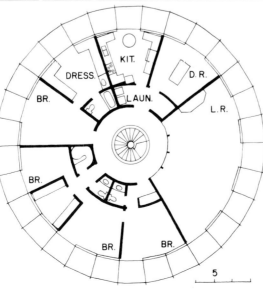

The key to turning a special shape into a workable house was the plan, and the key to a successful plan was provision of plenty of space, good circulation, and many special built-ins. The house is 72 feet wide, and pivots on the central staircase and hall for efficient circulation. A wide opening from living room to hall increases spaciousness, and, most importantly, provides immediate orientation when the house revolves. Service rooms are grouped at narrow ends of segments to leave the periphery mostly glass.

The Weese House

This frolicsome house should at least give pause to those who still cling to the belief that a modern house is typified by flat roofs and corner windows, or that contemporary as an architectural word implies any single style.

It is a house as comfortable as the ones our grandparents loved and built—and almost as full of the unexpected. Peaked roofs, sharply sloping ceilings, arched doorways, suspension bridges, catwalks, swings: all these and more are welded into a fresh, highly individual design. The architect planned it as a summer and winter weekend house for his family,

but by and large, it would make an admirable year-round house. In its design, Mr. Weese states that "the opportunity was taken to prove several theories of a more or less exploratory nature."

The house is situated to take full advantage of the five-acre wooded site, which is surrounded by lakes, and is constructed to form a saddle in the hilltop. The first floor is two and a half feet below grade at the flanks.

Architect and owner: Harry Weese. *Location:* Barrington, Illinois. *Contractor:* Rieke Construction.

Hedrich-Blessing photos

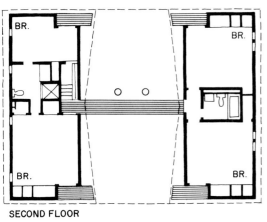
SECOND FLOOR

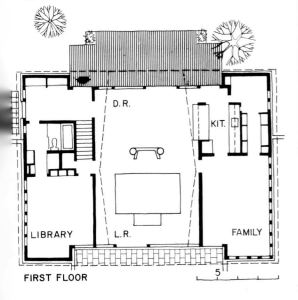
FIRST FLOOR

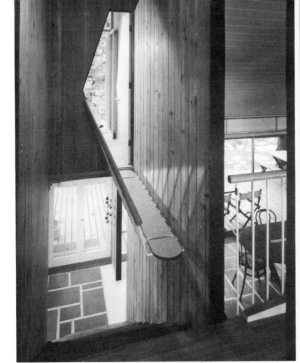
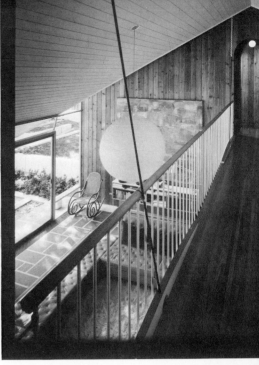

The main living area of the Weese house dominates the plan. It is big, with a pitched ceiling which rises the full two stories at its peak. It is divided visually into living and dining areas by a double fireplace. An informal "sitting well" increases the comfortable atmosphere on the living area side. The two-story gabled wings are connected by a dramatic bridge suspended by cables across this room. The wings house secondary living rooms and service areas on the main level, bedrooms above. A basement houses the laundry room, and a working area with drawing boards and benches for various activities in handicrafts.

The site is located in Barrington, Illinois, a small community about 60 miles northwest of Chicago. In planning the 2700-sq-ft house, all existing oak trees and most natural approaches were preserved. The land falls away on the swimming pool at the southwest (the living room side) to a lake below. Wood block paving continues outside the house on this side to surround the pool and help increase awareness of the natural setting. Sliding sash allow uninterrupted views and give easy access to the outdoors. A catwalk gives access to one child's bedroom. Each bedroom has a balcony reached from outside by a ladder—an idea prompted by a summer life involving swimming and sailing, and wet clothes.

The structure of the Weese house is basically a twin gabled one with the pitched ceiling of the main living area suspended between—not framed into them in the conventional way. Construction is of 4-in. double tongue and groove western red cedar plank—structure, insulation and finish being provided in the one material. The roof is of shingles. Materials were all selected for ease of maintenance, necessary in a household with young children.

A dimmer panel is located in the "sitting well" for the control of varying combinations of lighting to accentuate both interior and exterior features of the house.

The Wagener House

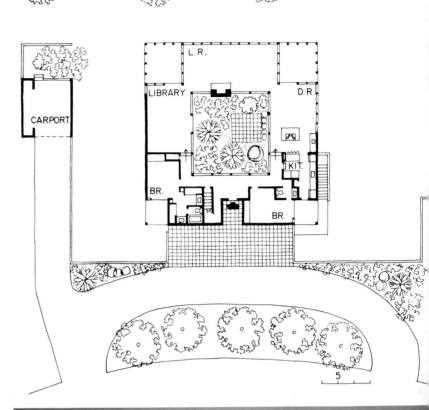

Hobart Wagener decided to compensate for the arid Colorado climate by planning his own house around an interior garden—beneath a 24-foot-square skylight. The result, as he describes it, is a rather "special environment where vines rather than walls are used to separate living areas." Although it will take some time for the plants to mature, the Wageners were surprised by the rapid rate of growth. Within a one-year period, they had 9-foot-tall poinsettias, many kinds of ferns and evergreens, as well as grapefruit, lemon and banana trees —in fact, many of the features of a tropical garden.

In a further effort to counteract the effects of the rather barren countryside, Wagener planned enclosed exterior spaces around the house. The landscaping was not yet complete when the photos were taken but is shown on the site plan, left. The fencing around the greater part of the property will be made of redwood-patterned-battens over cedar plywood to match the exterior wood surface of the house, and will in fact form an integral part of the front façade—considerably modifying the appearance.

The main living, kitchen and bedroom areas are disposed around the garden on the ground floor, but a balcony over the kitchen and bedroom areas provides two additional bedrooms, a bathroom and a study for the two teen-age children. A partial basement is included beneath the kitchen-dining room area.

The closed-in front or street façade is in sharp contrast to the back of the house where glass walls open to a view of an adjacent golf course to the south and west, with the Rocky Mountains in the background. The deep, sheltering roof provides physical and psychological protection in a climate of extremes.

Architect and owner: Hobart D. Wagener. *Location:* Boulder, Colorado. *Structural engineer:* W. B. Johnson; *contractor:* R. C. Grayson Construction Company.

Norman McGrath photos

The roof structure is as dramatic a feature inside the Wagener house as it is of the exterior. The simple, symmetrical composition of laminated wood beams and cedar decking is complemented by the wire-glass skylight area and the glass walls on the southern and western exposures.

The kitchen is divided into two areas, which can be separated by means of an oak folding door. In this way, the messy area can be closed off during meal-times, leaving the diners with a view of the rather attractive free-standing range and, as Hobart Wagener puts it, "the visually interesting part of food preparation."

The garden, which naturally enough is the main focus of the living areas, has its own central focus in the form of a brick island which makes an excellent base for sculpture, pottery or any kind of garden feature. A stone slab path leads through the garden to the island.

Furnishings are deliberately simple and elegant to avoid any conflict with the strongly articulated structure and plan of the building.

Gas-fired, forced-air heating and refrigerated cooling make for a comfortable environment at all seasons of the year.

The Schiffer House

An extremely strong and individualistic handling of the roof-ceiling formation characterizes Joseph Schiffer's design for his own house. Three wide, plywood box beams, supporting two bands of acrylic skylights, are the main elements in the roof structure. From the exterior, the two outer beams appear as wide roof 'channels' in which an unusual balance is established between the upward projections which support the skylight framing in the center of the roof, and the overhang along the sides of the house, which serves to shade the glass and give protection from excessive brightness and glare. The overhang is in turn balanced by an extension of the floor of the house to form an open porch going the whole way round the building.

The plywood roof beams are equally dominant inside the house, where they define each of the main living areas, and give an extraordinary sense of stability and permanence to the structure. Skylights running the full length of the house on either side of the center beam, throw light into the middle of all the living and family rooms and prevent the ceiling structure from appearing in any way heavy or oppressive.

Architect and owner: Joseph J. Schiffer. *Location:* Concord, Massachusetts. *Engineers:* William Thoen — Le Messurier & Associates. *Heating and Ventilating Consultant:* Victor Pesek. *Contractor:* Joseph Zaffina.

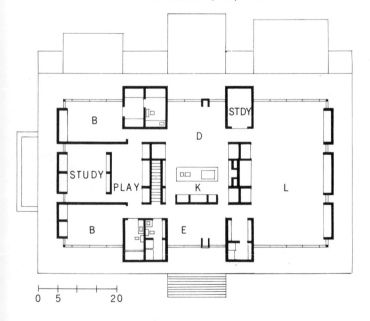

Joseph W. Molitor photos

Describing how the plan was evolved, Joseph Schiffer said: "The plan of the house is generated from the enclosure of all secondary functions, such as storage, closets, baths, and alcoves for the display or containment of works of art. The primary areas are the open living spaces created in between the closed walled forms of the secondary service areas." These U-shaped walls, which support the plywood box beams, are built of stud framing with plastic-faced plywood exterior surfaces and with a similar gypsum-plaster panel surface on the interior. This wall arrangement has the advantage of leaving room spaces clear and uncluttered and also of providing attractive alcoves for plants, pictures and small pieces of furniture. From the outside, the wall alcoves give an impression of solidarity to balance the bold expression of the roof structure. Glass areas between the alcoves give glimpses of the outdoors.

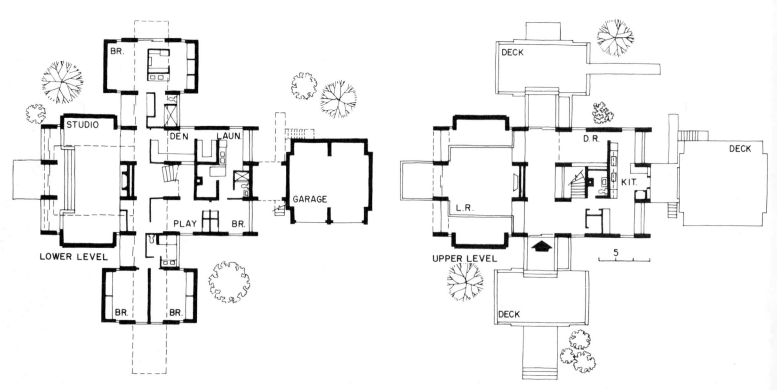

LOWER LEVEL

BR.

STUDIO

DEN   LAUN.

GARAGE

PLAY   BR.

BR.   BR.

UPPER LEVEL

DECK

D.R.

DECK

KIT.

L.R.

5

DECK

The Katselas House

This design exhibits a very striking interplay of room areas and structural materials. In designing the house for his own family, Tasso Katselas states that he outlined their four major requirements as: "1) a space worth living in; 2) a space answering diverse human needs, ranging from unrestrained expression to complete privacy; 3) a spatial order bold enough to accept the clutter and confusion of life, yet intimate enough to lend meaning to the smallest personal act; and 4) a space upon a slope, among giant oak trees, able to turn inward from nature's anger, able to pour outward toward nature's joys."

This rather unusual, yet admittedly comprehensive, program seems to have been well fulfilled. The house consistently holds one's interest, inside and out—cantilevers, balconies, domes, vaults, skylights, all combine to offer a considerable variety of spaces "bold and intimate." And the strong exterior forms seem comfortably at home on the wooded, irregular site.

The plan ramps down with the fall of the land, as can be seen in the photo of the entrance façade (opposite). All living and service areas are contained in the big central block of the house, with bedrooms and garages forming subsidiary wings on three sides. The roofs of each of the smaller wings are developed as sun decks, or, as over the children's bedrooms, an entrance terrace.

The most dramatic of the interior spaces is the two-story room devoted to living area and studio or family room. The living area is essentially a balcony jutting through the big room, and continuing to the outside as a cantilevered deck. Masonry "arms" provide clerestory lighting at each side of the room to balance the daylight from the window wall at the end. One enters the house on the upper level gallery where one is immediately faced with the vista of this projection of the living area into the tree tops. Family and entertaining spaces form a fairly open plan, with rooms for study, work and sleep closed off for privacy and quiet.

Architect and owner: Tasso Katselas. *Location:* Pittsburgh, Pennsylvania. *Structural Engineers:* R. M. Gensert Associates. *Contractor:* Thomas J. Plakidas.

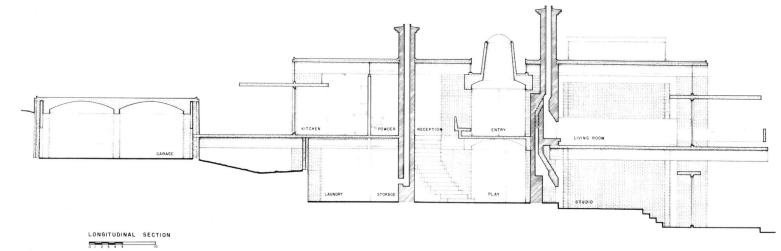

LONGITUDINAL SECTION
0 1 2 3 4 5   10

The sectional drawing of the Katselas house shows how the ceiling heights of the lower level are increased as the land falls from the garage wing to the tall studio. The brick and concrete structural materials are used as exposed interior finishes; construction is basically a series of solid brick piers, which support a series of poured-in-place arched beam slabs. Thus the concrete floor, ceiling and beam supports are accomplished in one process. One set of forms was used, spanning 9 feet in the short direction, 30 feet in the long direction. Cavity brick walls and glass were used as fill-in material between the piers. The glazing is installed in recesses poured into the concrete frame. The interior photos shown here include different views of the large living area and the dining area and the entrance gallery. All these spaces open to each other for an enormous sense of spaciousness. The cost of the house in 1963, excluding lot, landscape and furniture, was about $90,000. The heating is by a hot water, radiant panel system.

The Gregory House

This fanciful house achieves quite an air of distinction from its eye-catching double conoid roof. And the setting is quite appropriate to give such a scheme full play. The house is situated on a ten-acre site that has woods, fields and streams, and is far out in the country. The actual building site is set back about 800 feet from the road.

The double conoid roof is formed by two identical laminated wood beams on either of the long walls of the building. One is used upside-down in relation to the other. (A peak on one side is a valley on the other.) A straight laminated beam is at the center. The roof deck is made of white fir (2 by 3s) nailed to each other with 16d spikes 24-inches o.c. and to the beams with 20d spikes. The roof is freestanding supported by wood posts.

Full expression of the roof shape is emphasized by running all partitions only to a height of 7 feet, and keeping all of them non-bearing. Acoustic privacy is achieved by sheets of glass spanning from the partition tops to the roof decking. Stone walls give bracing and texture to the stucco and glass panels.

Architect and owner: Jules Gregory.
Location: Lambertville, New Jersey.
Building contractor: Karl Roos.

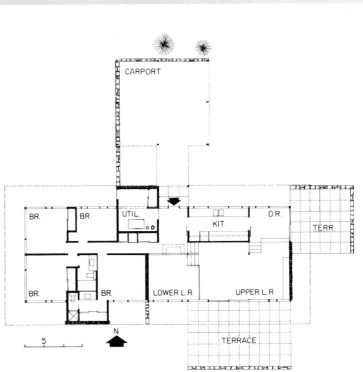

CARPORT

BR. | BR. | UTIL. | KIT. | D.R. | TERR.

BR. | BR. | LOWER L.R. | UPPER L.R.

TERRACE

5

N

153

Marc Neuhof photos

A slight drop in the site is used to give a multi-level scheme, with ceiling heights varied to the size of the rooms. Entrance, bedrooms, and kitchen-dining areas are on one level, with a step down to the main living area. Below this is a sort of contemporary inglenook with a fireplace. The flue from the fireplace passes underneath the entry slab (5 feet above the floor of the lower living room) and rises through the utility room adjacent.

Exterior walls are stucco and stone. Interior walls are stone and plaster. Floors are wood mosaic or tile. Doors are flush-panel plywood. The roof decking is covered with 1-inch insulation to receive the built-up tar and gravel roofing. Kitchen cabinets are plywood. The heating is by a warm air system.

Alexandre Georges photos

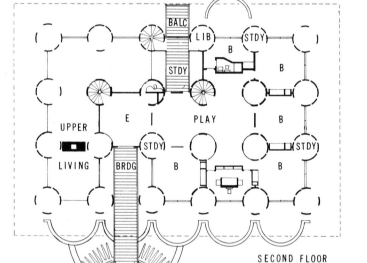

BALC
LIB STDY
B
STDY B
E PLAY B
UPPER
LIVING STDY BRDG STDY
B B B

SECOND FLOOR

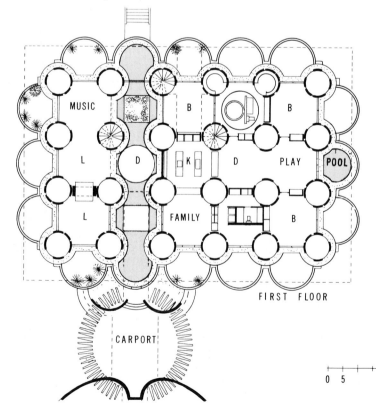

MUSIC
B B
L D
L D K D PLAY POOL
L
FAMILY B

CARPORT

FIRST FLOOR

0 5 20

The Portman House

John C. Portman's philosophy of architectural form and its use to modulate space and create special relationships between different kinds of spaces, has been embodied in this fascinating house, which he designed in 1965 for himself, his wife and family of six children. The creation of "space within space" was fundamental to his conception of his own house, and his concern was to create a number of closely defined spaces within a larger space, so that by relating the one to the other, one would gain an impression of the "continuous flow of space." Describing how these ideas were incorporated in the design and construction of the house, the architect said: "The house is created by composition of component parts, i.e. the curved cypress column walls, sliding doors, the shop-built cabinet walls etc. The space has been exploded creating a sense of the pavilion with a closing of cellular units for privacy as needed. A sense of the whole is felt in all the spaces."

Throughout the house the exploded columns appear in varying sizes and have a wide range of functions. Stairs, halls, study-rooms, closets, baths are all enclosed within them. Skylights above, and side openings admit light at unusual angles and prevent the spaces within the columns from seeming too enclosed. Outside the house the circular theme is repeated with brick-enclosed terraces, wading pools and flower beds.

The house is oriented so that the entrance axis is in a direct line to the skyline of the City of Atlanta 15 miles away. Entering the house on the second level, one is immediately conscious of the magnificent skyline

views. The indoor trees on the lower level form a perfect foil for the view. A water channel running through the living area provides another touch of visual excitement.

Visually and spatially exciting as it is, the house is also carefully planned for functional efficiency and the easy organization of the life of a large family. The living, formal dining, and master bedroom can be separated from the rest of the house by sliding walnut doors between the formal dining and kitchen areas. The kitchen is placed so that the children's activities in the family room, play area and wading pool can be easily supervised. The cost of the house in 1965 was about $165,000.

Architect and owner: John C. Portman, Jr. *Location:* Atlanta, Georgia. *Mechanical Engineer:* Britt Alderman, Jr. *Electrical Engineer:* Morris E. Harrison. *Contractor:* Sam N. Hodges, Jr., and Company. *Landscape Architect:* Edward L. Daugherty.

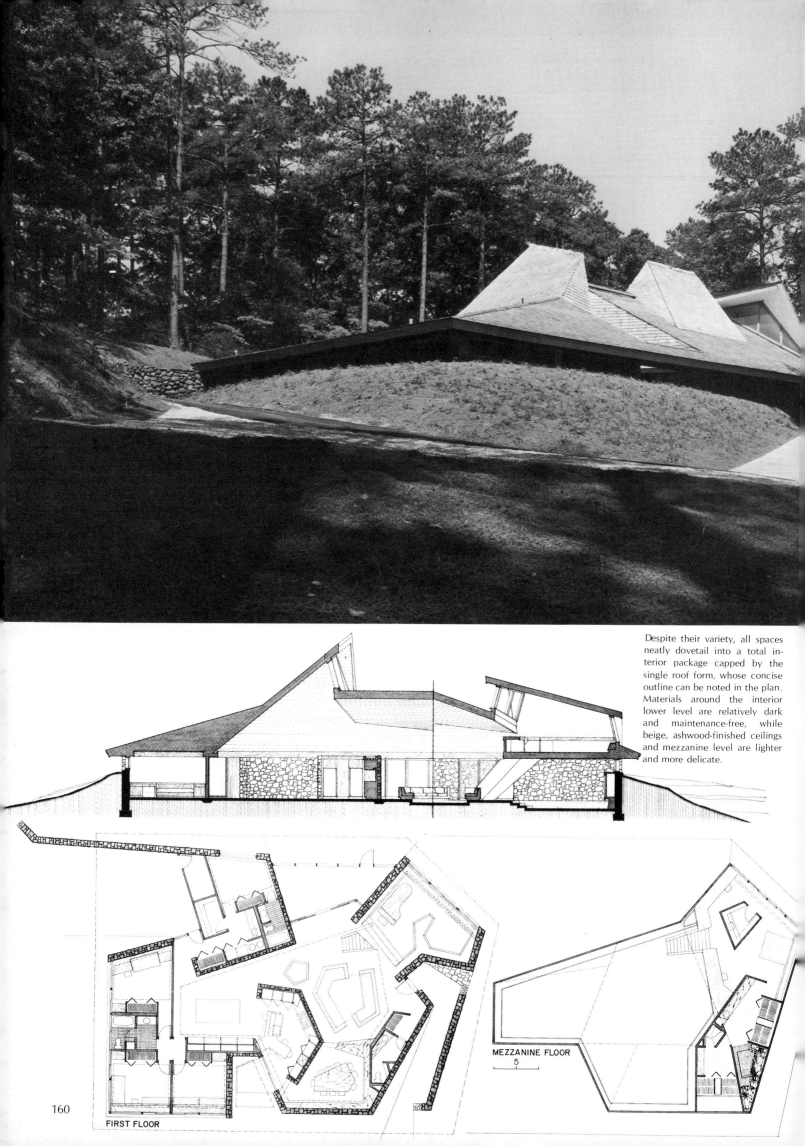

Despite their variety, all spaces neatly dovetail into a total interior package capped by the single roof form, whose concise outline can be noted in the plan. Materials around the interior lower level are relatively dark and maintenance-free, while beige, ashwood-finished ceilings and mezzanine level are lighter and more delicate.

FIRST FLOOR

MEZZANINE FLOOR

5

The Gruber House

The air of lively spaciousness that pervades this imaginative house is all the more remarkable as the house is half buried in the ground. Stone walls and cedar shingle for the roof combine with earth banks, or berms, to shape the unusual design. One of the restrictions the architect had to work with in designing for his own family was a site exposed to, and sloping up from, a well-travelled street corner. But he solved this problem with an originality evident throughout the design, in a scheme which integrates house and site outside, and creates inside a secluded world of light and air. Earth buttresses and stone walls are capped by the vaulted roof form, which reaches as high as 22 feet. Interior partitions, however, go only seven feet up, and all living areas share in the single overhead flow of space. Three light "scoops"—located over the master bedroom, dining room and family room—bring light to all parts. On gloomy days, recessed flood lighting is used.

Spaces—and "places"—are as practical as they are fun. Freed by the berm structure from planning the usual box-shaped rooms that conventional framing tends to dictate, the architect has carried through his own unorthodox concepts in a plan where, in his own words, the "well-defined spaces flow and interlock as do the functions within." To this end, the dining "room" is raised two steps above the living area, getting a view of the terrace beyond, and is defined by a built-in partition doubling as a buffet. The efficient kitchen is baffled from both, but opens onto the family/play room (the rectangular shape in the plan is a pool table). The master bedroom is set apart in its own mezzanine.

A terrace is carved out of the natural hill to let glass walls open for even more light, and for a secluded woodland view.

Architect and owner: Morton M. Gruber. *Location:* Atlanta, Georgia. *Contractor:* Burts Construction Company.

Erven Jourdan photos

Norman C. McGrath photos

SOLARIUM LEVEL

BEDROOM LEVEL

LIVING ROOM LEVEL

BRIDGE

DINING-KITCHEN LEVEL

STUDIO

Myron Goldfinger

The Goldfinger House

"A prototype for a prefabricated building system" is how Myron Goldfinger describes this house for his own family. Many young architects today, frustrated by their inability to constructively affect the housing crisis, use a similar rationale for the single-family residences they design. But few accomplish the poetic result Goldfinger has here.

The cedar-clad house is so intensely sculptural, inside and out, and so dramatically related to its rocky, wooded site that technical considerations seem to matter little. But as the photographs and drawings presented on these four pages indicate, it is a very complicated building, no matter how rational the basis of its design.

The basic module, 15 feet square, was determined by the standard 8- by 15-foot sliding glass door. This fenes-

tration contributes to the monumental scale of the house.

Another interesting aspect of the design approach, apparent especially in the photos above, is the assured and substantial way the house ties itself to the site, using the studio wing as an anchor. The section, overleaf, illustrates the ingenious method by which the architect provides a strong visual connection to the dining-kitchen floor yet acknowledges the change in grade. The view, right, of the bridge from the solarium emphasizes the smoothness with which the wing is joined to the main house. Other modules, if needed, may be added just as gracefully in the future, according to Goldfinger.

Architect and owner: Myron Goldfinger. *Location:* Waccabuc, New York. *Contractor:* John Sutton

Myron Goldfinger

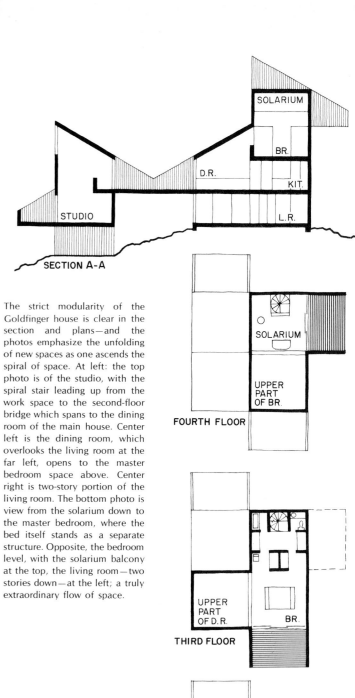

SECTION A-A

The strict modularity of the Goldfinger house is clear in the section and plans—and the photos emphasize the unfolding of new spaces as one ascends the spiral of space. At left: the top photo is of the studio, with the spiral stair leading up from the work space to the second-floor bridge which spans to the dining room of the main house. Center left is the dining room, which overlooks the living room at the far left, opens to the master bedroom space above. Center right is two-story portion of the living room. The bottom photo is view from the solarium down to the master bedroom, where the bed itself stands as a separate structure. Opposite, the bedroom level, with the solarium balcony at the top, the living room—two stories down—at the left; a truly extraordinary flow of space.

FOURTH FLOOR

THIRD FLOOR

SECOND FLOOR

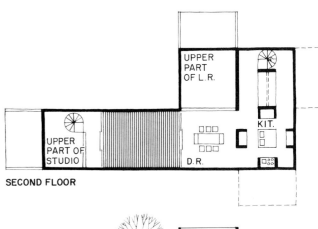

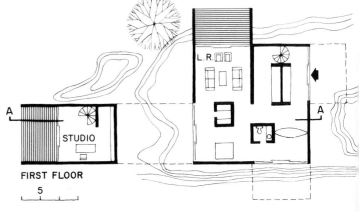

FIRST FLOOR

5

7

For some architects, like many clients, the city is the place, and rehab the solution.

Architect Peter Samton (his brownstone renovation is on page 168) says: "It is far easier being one's client on a brownstone renovation than starting a totally new house from scratch, even though we knew from the start we would have to gut the entire building. The interior was a rabbit-warren of rooms with little natural light and poor ventilation.

"The front of the house provided, probably, 90 per cent of the creative ability of the original architect back in 1890. So we kept as much of the façade intact as possible. The rear had no good features. Our solution was to create large open spaces with minimal construction inside, using a great deal of glass in the rear. The house is now filled with natural light and has a fine feeling of openness.

"I treated the job as if there were another client: my wife. And through her insistence we prevented some obvious mistakes. For example, I was quite content to have the washing machine and dryer in the cellar; she insisted it be up in the children's bathroom, on the same floor with the bedrooms. She also felt it was desirable to put the kitchen in the front of the house, facing the street, instead of putting it at the rear. Although we felt it was desirable for our children to play in the newly landscaped backyard, it turned out that they preferred to play in the street with the other children of the block. Therefore, supervision from the kitchen is a far easier task the way my wife figured it, rather than the way I figured it."

Architect Gordon Wittenberg, who remodeled an older house in an established neighborhood (page 172): "A special source of pleasure when you add on to an old house is that you constantly remodel the old house. This we do as we get ideas and as our living patterns change. Our family is now grown and seldom at home, so it gives us a whole new dimension for development. We only wish this sort of hobby were less expensive, because we are constantly getting in over our heads for things we probably don't need but just want to do."

The Samton House

The usual deficiencies of New York brownstones—narrow width and dark interiors—were present when owner-architect Peter Samton and his wife began renovating. They had a tight budget but wanted openness, daylight and as much flexibility in spatial and furniture arrangements as possible.

The width was fixed at 16'-2" by the enclosing party walls. The street elevation was established at the building line. But by demolishing a small existing extension of the building at the rear, and by substituting a generous window wall, natural light could reach deep into the waist of the building. Living spaces are therefore defined by furniture groupings rather than transverse walls.

Living room, kitchen, dining and work spaces occupy the parlor floor; sleeping quarters and playroom are below. A small, intimate court, at rear, extends the play space and furnishes a pleasant taste of outdoors. Completing this handsome renovation are two rental apartments above.

Architect and owner: Peter Samton (*partner,* Gruzen & Partners). *Location:* New York City. *Mechanical engineer:* Robert Freudenberg.

David Hirsch photos

In addition to flooding the main floor with light from the new greenhouse-like window wall, architect Peter Samton has added to the bright spaciousness of his renovated brownstone by a number of simple, but effective devices: creating a completely open plan with different "room" areas defined by low cabinets; using the same flooring throughout; exposing the original brick walls; and the selection of light, well-scaled furniture.

UPPER FLOOR   5   LOWER FLOOR

The Haid House

Architect David Haid's home for his family is inserted under the spreading oaks in a neighborhood of large Victorian houses. On a 50- by 150-foot lot, it has both privacy and openness, indoors and out.

The designer, an associate of Mies van der Rohe for several years, sees the house not so much as an expression of the Miesian style as use of a practical design vocabulary to solve a specific residential problem for a specific building lot.

The interior is open in plan except for the children's end which can be closed off. The rest of the house is a 50- by 40-foot space shared quite openly by the living and dining areas and the kitchen, and less so by the master bedroom. A large pantry—the round-ended shape near the middle of the plan—separates the vestibule and dining area. A curtain between the dining and living areas can be drawn during preparations for a dinner party but is more frequently moved around just for fun.

All sections of the house open onto courts which open to the spaces beyond (see plan) so there is a sense of containment rather than confinement. The expansive living room area (30- by 24-feet with the curtain drawn) opens onto a court formed by dense planting which, when fully grown, will make the house almost invisible from the street. This court is open on one side to the front walk. In the court off the kitchen and dining area there is a break in the wall to allow for the presence of a large oak. This break also provides glimpses into nearby yards. As the wall forming a play area outside the children's rooms is overlapped rather than attached, this space flows into the side yard.

The extraordinarily large, column-free, interior spaces were attained by the use of a steel frame roof resting on lead-padded bearing plates on the masonry walls. The glass walls are framed with shop fabricated steel units.

The colors of the structure, black steel fascias and mullions, beige terrazzo floors, gray buff brick walls and white drywall ceilings and partitions —contrast with the exuberant yellow divider curtain and golden orange master bedroom spread, both of Siamese silk.

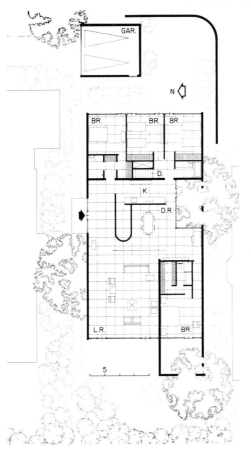

The interiors and the dining table and sofas were designed by the architect. Since the living room is exposed to the outdoors on three sides it is filled with light all day.

Bill Engdahl, Hedrich-Blessing photos

Architect and *owner:* David Haid. *Location:* Evanston, Illinois. *Structural engineers:* Wiesinger-Holland Ltd. *Mechanical and electrical engineers:* Wallace and Migdal. *Landscape architect:* Paul Thomas.

Frank Lotz Miller photos

The Wittenberg House

Using a typical, small cottage-style house on a corner lot as the secondary wing, architect Gordon Wittenberg designed this house for his own family in part to solve typical problems of adult-teenage zoning and added space. To this end, the adjacent lot was bought. By wrapping the addition, containing living areas and master bedroom suite, around the property to the setback line, the architect was, moreover, able to put to use outdoor space and gain privacy, light and variety of spaces the original house lacked. Glass-walled living and dining pavilions open up the house to the nearly-enclosed court, while the street-corner side of the new wing is closed off with a high stucco wall.

Architects and engineers: Witten-berg, Delony & Davidson, Inc. *Owner:* Gordon C. Wittenberg. *Location:* Little Rock, Arkansas.

A secluded dining terrace was formed by wrapping the new wing around it as a buffer from the street. The shop, formerly a garage, was integrated into the scheme by garden walls. Precious city trees were carefully preserved by the courtyard scheme. The old house (toned in plan), whose shuttered windows are visible in the photo below, survives as the children's wing.

The Jones House

The formal dignity of carefully massed masonry volumes fits nicely into a neighborhood of large old houses in mid-city Memphis. Walk Jones designed this house for one of six building lots developed from under-used back property. Not only did he have to take into account the quality of the established area but the fact that other new houses would be built either side of his, perhaps as close as ten feet.

As a result, the house opens front and back with the living and dining rooms facing the street, across which a planting strip assures a green vista. From the street the almost-symmetrical massing is enriched by the study block which emphasizes the location of the front door. The rear elevation is similar but an open patio on the first floor, this time with the enclosed space above, seems designed to draw the rear yard more readily into the family room. A tiny two-story enclosed courtyard on the north side (site plan and photos opposite), is used now as a play yard fully visible from the kitchen. In the future it will be a sculpture court.

Two seven-foot-wide strips containing all utilities and stairs, especially obvious in the site plan, separate the three major volumes of the house and provide a neat articulation for the functions within. In addition, the plan is divided on the first floor into the more formal portion to the street and the informal section to the rear centered around the fireplace in the family room.

Architect and owner: Walk C. Jones III of Walk Jones + Francis Mah, Inc. Location: Memphis, Tennessee. Mechanical engineers: Office of Griffith C. Burr. Interior design: Walk Jones + Francis Mah, Inc. Contractor: Larkey and Larkey Construction Co.

SECOND FLOOR   5

FIRST FLOOR

176

Otto Baitz photos

The Stubbins House

Hugh Stubbins has built a lively, walled-in retreat for himself and his wife, on Cambridge's historic Brattle Street. It stands amongst a long line of Georgian and other-styled houses going back to the house of Henry Wadsworth Longfellow and others of note. Though varied in design, all these houses now carry the general aura of "traditional". On the contemporary change of pace that this house introduces, Stubbins comments: "I wanted my addition to this street to be compatible, but also a reminder of its own era. It is essentially a house for a couple. The idea of the house is one that I have played with in one form or another over the years—it is like a barn with open lofts. In section its guideline geometry is a circle —a satisfying proportion."

The house can, indeed, almost be considered as a single room of very ample and satisfying proportions —with numerous alcoves and spaces that can be closed or left open as desired.

At first glance, the house appears relatively simple in concept, and its corner lot is well screened by an enclosing wall. However, a closer look reveals some of the surprising and intriguing details—all done with discernment and a good dollop of wit. Stubbins explains, "the main room soars 26 feet to the ridge; the structure, raised and dropped girts, ties and the like, are exposed to view. The simple, barn-like form is enlivened by punched holes in the walls for windows, in the roof for skylights; by overhanging the second floor at the ends; by a bay window, a dormer, by opening a whole wall; by hanging a louver for the western sun, and by pergolas and brick walls tying the house into the landscape. The visual secrets and surprises are not immediately revealed."

Architect and owner: Hugh Stubbins.
Location: Cambridge, Massachusetts.
Contractor: H. Tobiason.

Well-designed, well-executed details are a dominant highlight of the Stubbins house. Though some of them are highly individual (note the shuttered "windows" from the upstairs bedrooms into the main room, and the open balcony "hallway"), all also evidence a great love for good materials and finishes. Stubbins comments that the "materials were selected for beauty, simplicity and ease of maintenance. The exterior is rough-sawn redwood, white-painted window trim, asphalt shingles (the building code required fire rating), and waterstruck brick for walls and the terrace around the swimming pool.

"On the interior, the structural Douglas fir is stained dark brown. Dining room and kitchen floors are Welsh tile—the color of old leather; wide oak boards form the floors of the living room, and the entire second floor is carpeted." To highlight these materials, all walls and ceilings are simple rough plaster, painted white, with well-placed accent lights.

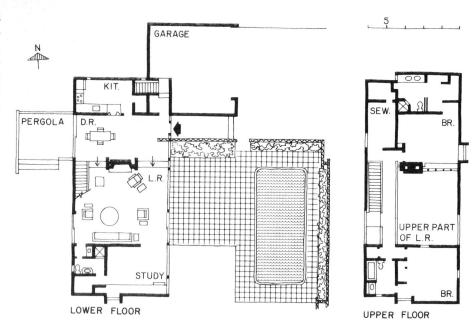

LOWER FLOOR

UPPER FLOOR

Louis Reens, photos

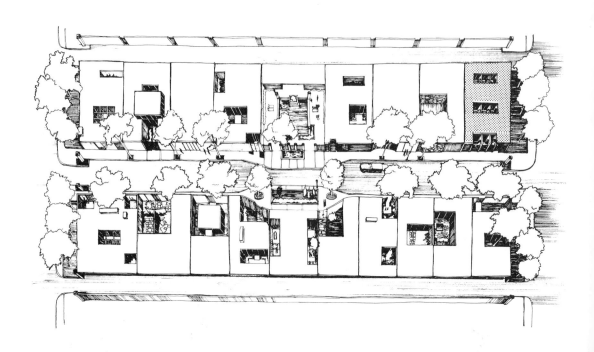

The Bolton House

The traditional "townhouse" concept has been successfully revived in this southern house, one of a group of custom-designed row houses for a Houston development planned by the architect. Stylistically, the houses are all quite contemporary, but the use of similar and fairly traditional materials gives a unified, almost "timeless" quality.

The development is built in the midst of a typical city subdivision which has large lawns and traditional houses built out to 10 foot restriction lines at the sides of each lot. By planning this new development as a unit, it was possible to extend the encompassing walls of each house to the lot lines. A communal swimming pool and recreation pavilion are placed at the center of the development. Service alleys range the back of each block of houses.

This house is built on a corner lot of the area, on a site measuring 45 by 75 feet. To minimize the space required, a carport was devised for parking sideways at the back, off the service alley. Vistas are provided for each room inside the house by a series of patios formed by colonnades of brick arches. The arches carry through the house as a design motif.

Architect and owner: Preston M. Bolton. *Location:* Houston, Texas. *Structural Engineer:* R. George Cunningham. *Contractor:* Stewart & Stewart Construction Company.

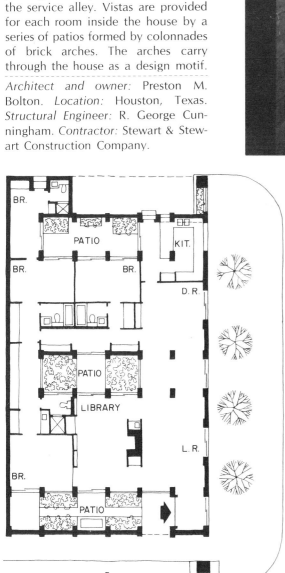

Behind the 12-foot-high paneled doors at the entrance of the Bolton house lies a series of rooms with a startling sense of spaciousness—a quality which is unfortunately not adequately conveyed by the photographs. The owners state that: "People are continually amazed that we have four bedrooms and four baths, each with its own patio view in this limited space, but the living area of our house has been considerably increased by the garden courts. We have small bedrooms and this is the way we like to live—with a minimum of furniture and maximum use of organized dress-ing room storage. Our favorite place is the library with its walls of books and glass: one way we look out on a patio with a fountain of playing water; the other way, to a tropical garden with swaying palms. We like our house and wouldn't change a thing."

The interior organization of the house is also a very conveniently and flexibly arranged one. For example, the library is placed where it may be used with the living area for entertaining, or with the master bedroom to form a private apartment. The library and living room are divided by a fireplace enclosed in natural

finish walnut with white divider strips.

The kitchen is placed for direct service in the living-dining area or the rear patio, and adjoins the carport to ease the handling of groceries and deliveries. The maid's quarters at the back also have an entrance through the rear patio, which doubles in function as a children's play area. The child's bedroom, bath and dressing room open both from the maid's room and the master bedroom corridor to afford surveillance. The fourth bedroom, bath and dressing room, forms a guest suite. Along the side of the house flanking the public street, are a series of arched windows, shielded by walnut shutters to allow complete privacy or openness, as one desires.

The structure of the house is wood

Edward A. Bourdon photos

frame on a concrete slab, with exterior walls of champagne-colored Mexican brick and concrete block. Interior walls are white-painted wall board, brick and walnut paneling; floors are dark oak with borders of white tile.

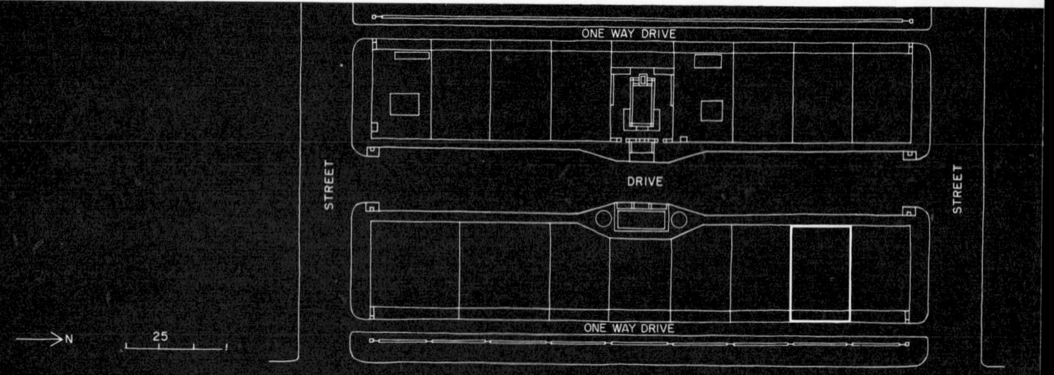

Alexandre Georges photos

The Sobel House

This elegant, unusually spacious little town house, designed by architect Robert Sobel for himself and his wife, heralds the completion of a remarkable block of privately built, custom-designed houses. Conceived of and started by another Houston architect, Preston Bolton, a little over a decade ago—the block has been brought to fruition by a strong act of will, by all concerned, to follow the original ideas. The houses, which line two sides of a private street, are all one story and built of a similar brick—with major exterior variances only in discreet patterns in the brick-work, in the thin roof coping, and in the front doors. The block has a central, communal swimming pool and recreation pavilion; carports and service alleys are behind each row of houses. By planning the development as a unit, full use of each lot was possible—with each house gaining light and air from internal courts.

The Sobel house, shown here, possibly has the most open interiors of all the group—being essentially planned as a single room around a garden. Provision *is* made, however, for achieving privacy when desired.

As can be noted in the plan, all principal rooms—entry, living room, dining room and master bedroom—have glass walls flanking the court; even the two study/guest-bedrooms are afforded a corner peek at the foliage. A system of shutters ranging the living room and bedroom sides of the court provides sun control and privacy when needed. Unity of all these spaces is emphasized by white plasterboard walls throughout, and by using a single flooring material—a deep purple iron-spot brick—for all rooms, and also for paving in the garden court.

An extra note of spatial drama is added by variations in ceiling heights: most are ten feet, with the entry dropped two feet to emphasize the general spaciousness; at the back of the compound, the dining room ceiling unexpectedly rises in a pyramidal form to a six-foot skylight.

SOBEL RESIDENCE, Houston, Texas. *Architect and owner:* Robert Sobel. *Engineers:* Krahl and Gaddy (structural). *Contractor:* Orval Burke.

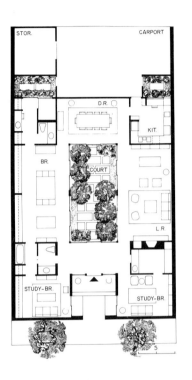

On a 45- by 78-foot buildable lot, architect Sobel has created a house with a great sense of privacy from the outside, and a great flow of space and openness in the interiors. In addition to the central garden court, on which all principal rooms focus, there are little gardens at the entry (right), which also serve the guest bedrooms, and off the master bath and the kitchen (bottom right).

To help unify the sense of continuous space in the house, Sobel has used quiet, natural materials for the furnishings throughout: teak, walnut, rosewood, travertine, leather. Bright accents are supplied by rugs and accessories. There are two small studies flanking the entry, that double as guest bedrooms (far right). The master bedroom is a luxurious 26 feet long at present (bottom right), but can be divided into two bedrooms in the future.

8

In some cases, small details, or big intangibles, make the difference

In John Carden Campbell's house (page 28): ". . . the great feeling of spaciousness is due to the 12-foot ceiling. While this particular factor more or less 'makes the house,' it cost only about $300 more than standard 8-foot ceilings."

Says architect Paul Damaz of his weekend house (page 196): "The quality of interior light was a major concern and is probably the most successful aspect of the house. The north orientation creates a soft, uniform light which penetrates the most remote areas of the house. Windows are located in such a way that, from sunrise to sunset, moving splashes of sun strike the living area, always in different places according to the time of day and time of the year. Hard glaring sun is not admitted. Curtains or blinds are not necessary. Bedrooms are oriented east to admit the morning sun. The kitchen is oriented west and receives the sun during the late afternoon cooking time. . . . It is easy to design a flashy, daring house which will look stunning in a color publication. It is something else to design a house where your body and soul fit like a snail in its shell."

Some houses seem right because of details that seem to make special sense for no special reason. Says Architect Rem Huygens of his house (page 210): "The unusual structural system was worked out one day at lunch—on a paper napkin. Some of the main characteristics of the house, such as the battered concrete walls, the rows of French doors, and the glass gables, we never repeated in other houses. I could not say what the reason for this is. I may use them again someday, if it seems appropriate."

Gil Amiaga photos

The Moger House

In this weekend and vacation house, architect Richard Moger displays as much skill in creating distinctive architecture with minimal size and budget as he has previously shown with more ample resources.

Though the house itself contains only 1500 square feet, and was built for $35,000, an illusion of far greater size—even luxury—has been created by some intriguing design techniques. The most obvious ones are the use of a modified "open plan," and the allocation of the greater part of the house to a big living room and minimal (but ample) spaces for other areas. These ideas, of course, have been around for quite a while, but here they have been combined with a highly successful interplay of scale,

light, openness and seclusion, which gives the sense of variety so often tragically lacking in a small house. In addition, Moger has incorporated an eye-catching *leitmotif* of rectangles and curves, all tied together by highly accented diagonal focal points; this, in the best sense, is the "decorative" element in the house—very simple, very architectural, with no frills, fuss or ostentation—and is obvious in the structure, the furnishings, even the wall hangings. This visual use of the diagonal (as can readily be seen in the photographs) increases the perspective and sense of visual space to a remarkable degree.

Though, when all doors are open, one can see—or at least be conscious of—most all of the spaces in the house

(and all these spaces somehow take advantage of the big, east-facing glass wall of the living area), necessary privacy is assured by doors to bedroom, baths, kitchen, and tracks provided for curtains, if they are desired, at the windows.

In part, the budget was met by simple construction: a wood frame on concrete block foundation, cedar siding, painted gypsum board intetiors, built-up roof, quarry tile floors, furnace in outside-access crawl space. All is neat, easy to maintain.

Architect and owner: Richard R. Moger. *Location:* Southampton, New York. *Engineers:* Langer & Polise (mechanical); Paul Gugliotta (structural). *Contractor:* John Caramagna.

Basically rectangular in shape, the house gains character by some simply achieved, but highly rhythmical undulations of walls to express the activity areas and functions occurring inside. The combined sense of shelter and openness that occurs within is also expressed in the relatively closed entrance facade (across-page), the glass at back (far left and below).

Details throughout are simple, unobtrusive, well proportioned, with spaces and massing given importance; even on a limited budget, there is no deference to the "expose all the working innards" school—the mechanics of the house are not seen.

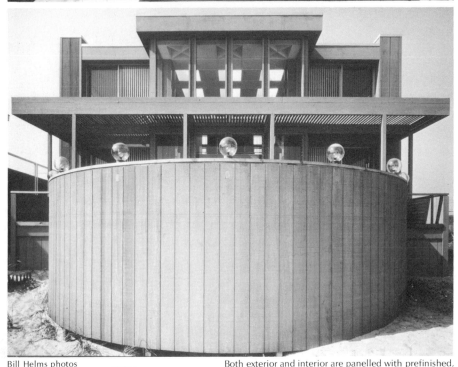

The Combs House

Architect Earl Combs' Fire Island beach house has a Palladian presence with its symmetry, substantiality and dominant central two-story entry way and living room. Within the overall box-like configuration this formality is reinforced by the reiteration of the square. The unglazed ceramic, mosaic tile flooring pattern is a projection of the square coffers and skylights. The columns and rooms are square, as are the basic forms of the dining and coffee tables, and the built-in seating, all designed by the architect.

Although the house is very enclosed on three sides, to assure privacy on the narrow 60- by 30-foot lot, it is actually filled with light. All rooms receive light from at least three directions. All but the living room have strip windows just below the ceiling, spanning from column to column; the baths and kitchen each have three.

The two-story skylighted living room becomes a light well for the adjoining study and dining room and the bedrooms above, which have sliding glass doors overlooking it. Mirrored sliding glass doors on the bathrooms, with their reflected views of the sea, are like internal windows. And the predominantly white floors throughout provide an additional source of reflected light. All this internal light balances glare from the beach side of the house, which has floor-to-ceiling fixed glass or sliding glass doors all the way across.

Structurally the house is a variant of post and beam construction. The foundations are 6- by 6-foot posts driven 12 feet into the sand all the way down to the water. The columns are square and hollow consisting of four corner posts covered with a stiffening skin of plywood. Some columns house mechanical equipment but most are storage units provided with door panels having touch latch hardware. In the kitchen this eliminates all wall-hung cabinets, creating more open work surfaces. In the living room a four-speaker sound system is built into the columns.

The ship's portholes in the bathrooms and the beach facade with deck and sunscreen resembling the bow and bridge of a ship seem quite at home next to the pounding surf.

Architect and owner: Earl Burns Combs. *Location:* Fire Island Pines, New York. *Contractor:* Joseph Chasas.

Bill Helms photos

Both exterior and interior are panelled with prefinished, gray-stained plywood. Ceilings and exterior trim above the strip windows are of plastic-coated hardboard. The coffee table and built-in seating fit into the floor pattern, and the floor stripes meet and match in width the expression of the corner posts in each column, evidence of thorough detailing.

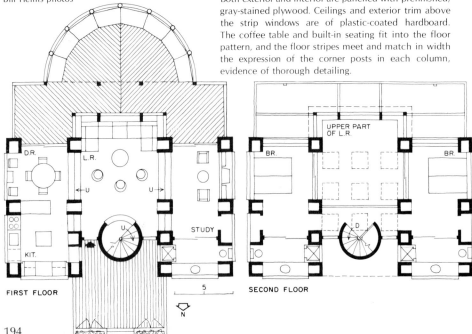

FIRST FLOOR

5

SECOND FLOOR

N

George Cserna photos

Paul Damaz

Simple wood-framed and ply-wood clad volumes provide a lively interplay of form and shadow throughout the day. A trellis at the entrance and the guest-house provide varying degrees of spatial enclosure outdoors. Indoors a well-placed window bathes the living room wall with afternoon sun. The hexagonal brick pavers are used both indoors and on the terrace.

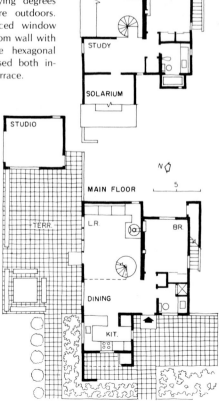

SECOND FLOOR

BR.

STUDY

SOLARIUM

STUDIO

N

MAIN FLOOR

5

TERR.

L.R.

BR.

DINING

KIT.

196

The Damaz House

Looking north across a large field surrounded by trees, this sculptural vacation house has a site similar to many in eastern Long Island. Because of the immense popularity of the area as a New York City recreation spot, land costs along water's edge are extremely high. Thus, many modest houses are sited on agricultural land or in the woods. Paul Damaz has used a two-story, north-facing living room to tie the floors together into one free-flowing space. With the exception of bedrooms and baths, all the interior spaces are open to each other. Care has been taken to place windows where they catch the morning and late afternoon sunlight. The tub in the master bath, in its own little turret, far left above the trellis, has a window specially placed for watching the sunset while bathing. A small separate structure to the northeast serves as a studio and guest house. The house is filled with works by artists whom Annie Damaz represents, including paintings, sculpture and prints.

Architect and Owner: Paul Damaz, of Damaz and Weigel. *Location:* East Hampton, N.Y. *Contractor:* William Lynch.

The Fitzpatrick House

Chameleon-like, the reflective bronze glass walls of this elegantly wood-framed house change appearance with the seasons, and add a considerable degree of internal privacy and glare control. Architect Fitzpatrick professes that he is fascinated by small French pavilions, and he has been extremely successful here in creating a contemporary version of one using today's most modern materials and equipment.

The serene, precisely designed house is set on a grass terrace, and approached along a rising curved gravel drive to a court formed against the hillside. Views expand in all directions over meadows and woods.

Inside, the house has considerable spatial and visual interest, as well as areas of quiet and privacy. The main living area, which measures 20 by 45 feet, is two stories high at its center. Balconies overlook it on three sides and add spaces for study, art studio and a connecting gallery to display paintings by the architect. The combination of glass walls looking outward, low- and high-ceilinged areas, balconies and alcoves greatly increases the sense of spaciousness, and the usefulness of the house. The bronze glass and white color scheme of the exterior also forms the basic theme for the interiors, sparked by bright primary colors of the paintings and linen cushions on chairs and benches. Most of the furniture was specially designed for the house by the architect. The main rooms were planned for comfortable country living and for frequent entertaining.

Structurally, the house is especially noteworthy for the visual slenderness of its wood frame—an illusion created by extending the thin-edged supports inwards for the needed strength, and by insetting the floor and roof supports well behind the bronze-toned glass.

Architect and owner: Robert E. Fitzpatrick. *Location:* Yorktown, New York. *Engineers:* Tege Hermansen (structural), Douglas Gawman (mechanical). *Interior design:* Mary Fitzpatrick.

FIRST FLOOR   SECOND FLOOR   5

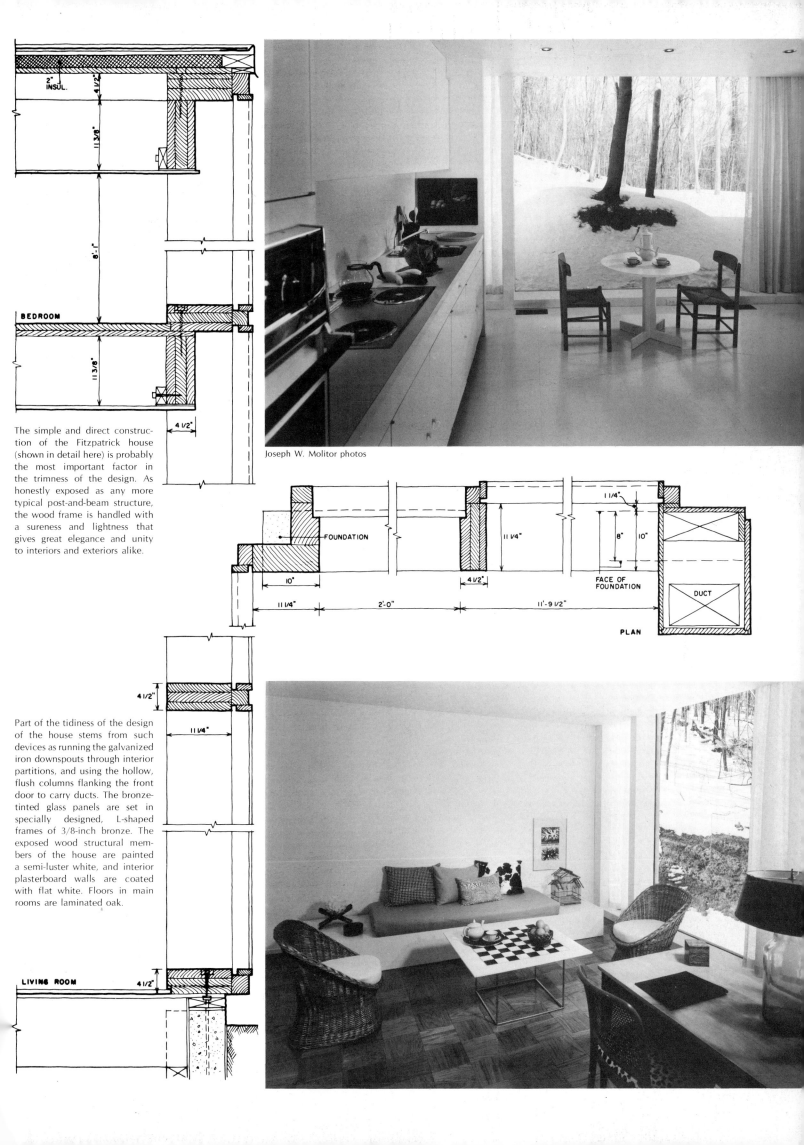

2"
INSUL.

4 1/2"

11 3/8"

8'-1"

BEDROOM

11 3/8"

4 1/2"

The simple and direct construction of the Fitzpatrick house (shown in detail here) is probably the most important factor in the trimness of the design. As honestly exposed as any more typical post-and-beam structure, the wood frame is handled with a sureness and lightness that gives great elegance and unity to interiors and exteriors alike.

Joseph W. Molitor photos

FOUNDATION

11 1/4"

10"

4 1/2"

11 1/4"

8"

10"

FACE OF FOUNDATION

DUCT

11 1/4"

2'-0"

11'-9 1/2"

PLAN

4 1/2"

11 1/4"

Part of the tidiness of the design of the house stems from such devices as running the galvanized iron downspouts through interior partitions, and using the hollow, flush columns flanking the front door to carry ducts. The bronze-tinted glass panels are set in specially designed, L-shaped frames of 3/8-inch bronze. The exposed wood structural members of the house are painted a semi-luster white, and interior plasterboard walls are coated with flat white. Floors in main rooms are laminated oak.

LIVING ROOM

4 1/2"

The Ossipoff House

The almost never-never-landish quality of the climate and landscape in our newest state has a very suitable counterfoil in this comfortable and casually relaxed house, by one of the Islands' best known architects for his own family. From the road, and from the sea, it gently suggests itself in the lush palm grove. Yet within, spacious and skillfully detailed and patterned areas establish an equally pleasant atmosphere.

One of the most effective features of the house, and one which greatly adds to its sense of space, is its unusual ceiling, whose continuous plane extends through to the outdoor terrace roofs. Its striped effect is caused by application of wood plank over fiberboard, and was done with the idea of achieving warmth of wood, simultaneously with broken surface, and some exposure of the fiberboard for acoustic purposes. On the result, the architect states: "It has worked."

The long, informally disposed plan is arranged so that all major living areas have a view of the sea. Attractively planted courts at the entrance and at the center of the house provide more intimate views for the master bedroom, guest room, and living room.

Architect and owner: Vladimir N. Ossipoff. *Location:* Honolulu, Hawaii. *Landscape Architect:* George Walters. *Contractor:* S. Mivra.

Robert Wenkam photos

The plan of the Ossipoff house includes an array of places for dining.
A secondary lanai area (behind garage, off dining room) provides a
place for outdoor cooking out of the
wind, which comes from the northeast. The kitchen has a dining corner
where the family eats on the maid's
day off. The architect refers to the
large undesignated space between
the study and the entrance gallery
as a "glory-hole sans ceiling"!

The structure permits the continuous plane of ceiling through use of
open-web steel joists as ridge and
door headers within 2-by-12 in. framework. The foundation is concrete,
and exterior walls are hollow cement
block, painted. The roof is corrugated
cement-asbestos.

Materials are, for the most part,
given a natural finish. Living room
ceilings are redwood, floors are clay
tile. Kitchen floors are vinyl tile and
clay tile; baths are vinyl or cork tile.
Interior walls are glass, gypsum board
or teak. Bathroom counters are marble.

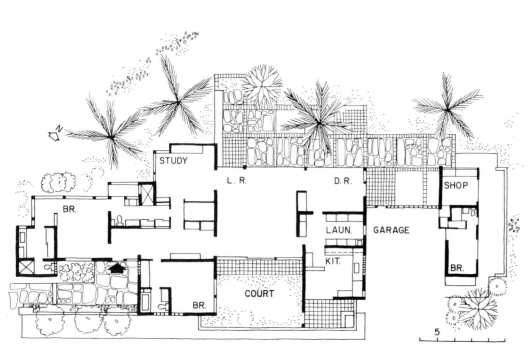

205

The Gibbs House

The design of this house began with some deed restrictions—which (in addition to the requirement that the fence, if any, be three-rail, white) called for a shingle roof and white walls. Within this arbitrary discipline, architect Gibbs—for his own house—set his own discipline: an extraordinary effort to, in his own words, "design away the detail." And this effort has indeed established the character of the house. There is, for example, no trim inside or out—fixed glass panels are slip glazed into the plaster or ceiling recesses, and the glass doors (which ride in specially shaped head and sill tracks) slide into pockets built into the walls (see plans). The interior doors have no jambs, heads, or sills—but pivot on floor and ceiling and are stopped by half-inch changes in the wall plane.

This attention to detail fits into a most disciplined basic concept: a dark ceiling plane (stained redwood) and a dark floor plane (wool carpet) that provide limits for the strong white element of the plaster walls. Says Gibbs: "A conscious attempt was made to resolve the walls into many clean tectangular planes and forms—and furnishings, people and plants look well against them."

The house is framed in wood—and the details "respect the notion that it is either expensive or impossible to get finished wood joinery or detail work in the field." The plan offers the downhill views of the city and ocean to the living room, the master bedroom, and the courtyard framed by these rooms. But all rooms—by use of the panels of glass and screening—can be as open (or as closed) as the family wishes to the yard, the breeze and the outdoors.

Architects: Donald Gibbs & Hugh Gibbs. *Owner:* Donald Gibbs. *Location:* Palos Verdes Peninsula, California *Landscape architect:* Bettler Baldwin. *Interior design:* Donald Gibbs. *Contractor:* Lyman Merril.

On the exterior, the rough shingle roof, the unadorned plaster walls, and the glass openings are all treated in a manner that is thoroughly contemporary, but fits comfortably in a conservative neighborhood. Inside, the same sense of big planes of material exists—but all is warmed by the light and the views, and the strongly contrasting framework of ceiling and floor. The kitchen, (far right, bottom) is designed as a "living place, not just a work place"—it is carpeted, with teak cabinets and work tops. And everywhere, the 10-foot-high ceilings add a sense of space and dramatize the painstaking attention to detail.

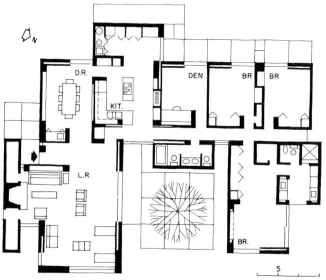

Wayne Thom photos

When deed restrictions require the design of a new house to "relate to its historic neighbor", a contemporary-minded architect building for himself has to exert even more ingenuity than usual to reconcile the two points of view. Remmert Huygens has achieved this in a straightforward manner by exploiting "rustic" qualities of contemporary materials.

The new house is located on a wooded, hillside site in Wayland, Massachusetts, and looks over the Sudbury River valley and towards the hills of New Hampshire. Across the street is the historic neighbor to which the house had to be related:

a large white frame residence and red barn, built in the 18th century as an inn on the post route to New York.

Huygens' own program required virtually a one-room house, with a studio which could later be converted into two children's bedrooms, and a dressing room which could become a second bathroom. An in-line floor plan was desired to give all rooms morning sun, as well as some share of the view to the west.

The concept of the house was determined by simple and clearly defined elements: a number of separate, battered concrete wall masses, and a tent-like, cedar-shingled roof. Huy-

gens has commented that, "the advantage of being one's own architect is that it is possible to take one single, simple idea, build it, and carry it through without being forced into any compromise or elaboration." Here, to accentuate the voids between the unrelated wall masses, all openings have French doors made of thin rolled-steel sections. The battered walls give horizontal bracing for the roof.

Architects: Huygens and Tappé. *Location:* Wayland, Massachusetts. *Owner:* Remmert W. Huygens. *Structural engineers:* Souza and True. *Contractors:* Osmond Brothers.

The Huygens House

Phokion Karas photos

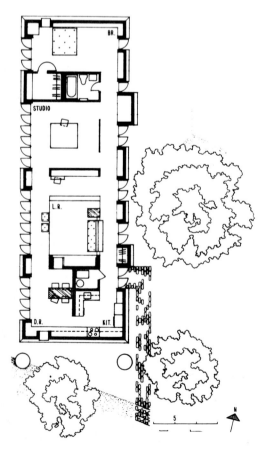

The Coplans House

Patricia Coplans' hillside house in San Francisco rises in a conspiracy of angled planes and projections to overlook Golden Gate Park and the Pacific Ocean. The projecting bay windows are part of a local residential tradition but the sloping window walls are a direct response to particular site conditions and the architect-owner's desire to capture as much sunlight as possible on this steeply contoured north slope.

The plan is compact and simply ordered in spite of the visual complications created by the projections. The living room occupies the north end of the house over the garage and is overlooked, in turn, by a gallery level guest bedroom. Master bedroom and bath occupy the second floor over the kitchen. The sloping glass roof of the dining area frames a view up the slope of tall stands of eucalyptus. A central entry hall, also skylighted, is reached from the garage below or by a winding outdoor stair on the west side of the house.

Finish materials are sympathetically selected and detailed with skill. Exterior walls are western cedar nailed up in diagonals that echo the slope of the site in two directions. Interior partitions are gypsum board over wood studs; flooring is teak parquet for the living room and clay tile for dining room and kitchen. Rich accents, like the marble fireplace surround, are used sparingly. A dark red baked enamel finish, used on all gutters, downspouts, window sash corner details and roof, contrasts warmly with the cedar siding, and gives the house a crisp, firm-edged angularity. This linear emphasis is restated inside in the window and door trim as in the unusually crisp and elegant skylight details.

The Coplans house is invested with a stimulating spatial character—a character that is personal but not aberrant, a character that does not dissolve with the second or third look.

Architect and owner: Patricia A. Coplans of Burger and Coplans. *Location:* San Francisco, California. *Engineers:* Geoffrey Barrett (structural); James Peterson (mechanical). *General contractor:* Patricia Coplans.

Edmund Burger

Edmund Burger

The furnishings in the Coplans' house are a mixture of built-ins and modern classics in chrome, cane and leather. The relative formality of many of these pieces is surprising but no problems of compatibility seem to arise.

Large skylights in many spaces flood the house with light but glazing is tinted for protection against the sun's direct rays.

9

And sometimes unique problems create some of the most interesting houses of all

Architect Arthur Cotton Moore's extraordinary house (page 220) grew from one kind of unique problem. He writes: "I think that most architects' natural state of having very little in the way of funds causes them to wind up purchasing some odd-shaped, strange lot that is a bargain, hoping that their imagination will be able to overcome the difficulties of the site. Sometimes the adversity is a stimulus to design. In the case of our house, the stimulation was extreme." Indeed it was, and his long letter to the editors of this book is reproduced here—both because it is fun to read and because it shows that an able architect, working within the most rigid of restraints, can create the kind of house that just doesn't happen except with skilled hands and a great deal of thought:

"Our house project began when I observed, on a project I was doing for a client, that there were four tiny leftover triangular pieces of land (which also were of a different zoning) at the far corner of the estate. From an economic perspective, since it was situated in a desirable area, the 2,000 square feet was worth very little money or quite a lot, depending on its usability. Moreover, the location was convenient to my office (six blocks), and to the full range of downtown Washington.

"The challenge was to see if indeed one could place any kind of house on the incredibly irregular, acutely triangular lot, further compounded by the fact that it was also essentially a cliff. It looked like a leftover bramble patch perched on the side of a steep embankment. The form of the house grew out of these adversities. There was the need to shape the house as a series of steps or terraces to minimize a fantastic retaining wall, and also get it at an elevation where it would receive some sunlight and not be masked by the adjacent house. It was also our fond hope that even though this was a miniature lot, we could try to create a kind of a walled enclave, a totally interior type of place, which would concentrate on a small swimming pool, a rather unique feature since Georgetown is made up of 20-foot-wide rowhouses and 20-foot-deep yards, practically precluding pools. Beyond the usual problems of trying to fix a house to the edge of a cliff where the soil condition is poor, there were unique legal problems.

"First, the zoning regulations were a problem as the very shape of the lot defined the standard setback rules, and required special interpretation by the zoning board. Because, in a legal zoning sense, I was building in a rowhouse district, I would be permitted to build a house on as little as 2,000 square feet only if it met the definition of a rowhouse. The districting line passes through the lots, meaning that not all of the lot is rowhouse. The definition of a rowhouse is that it goes from side lot line to side lot line, although it doesn't necessarily have to abut another house. This meant that we would have to fill out the whole length of a portion of the triangle so that the house would be 4 feet wide at one point, and 30 feet wide at the other end. It also meant that the front of the house would have to be 80 feet long— a very long façade indeed. Georgetown is under the jurisdiction of the Fine Arts Commission of Washington, which expects houses in the area to be essentially 20-foot-wide rowhouses of Colonial design. Although I was certainly only going to build a contemporary house, I could not even refer as precedent to any analogous Colonial 80-foot rowhouse. At one point, after several years, I facetiously suggested to the Fine Arts Commission that I simulate four rowhouse façades, each 20 feet wide along the street. They finally let me go ahead with a long, essentially blank exterior. We, of course, desired the exterior to be relatively blank, both for security and because the idea of the house was the internalization of a private walled space. Because of the shape of the lot, the design response had to be a series of triangular forms, yet the Fine Arts Commission insisted that, from the exterior, the house appear square to the street on both public sides. The notion became to treat the house from the exterior as a section of wall, tied into a new wall on the large estate next door. The next-door owner reworked a section of his estate to merge with our wall-house— tearing down some unsightly corrugated tin garages—so that we would create a simple uniform appearance to the street. In this way, I felt that a new, albeit contemporary, house would fit in with minimal impact to the neighborhood. The problem, obviously, of a structure appearing to be orthogonal when in fact it is a series of triangles, meant real structural difficulties. At a point about halfway through the living room the directions of structure change, and therefore all mechanical work had to change directions. Also, because of the intense tightness of the lot, to fit a pool in legally and to achieve a sense of spaciousness in the living room, I had to cantilever the living room over the pool, which meant that all the structure and mechanical lines on most of the back side of the house had to come down on the diagonal cantilever and then be transferred back.

"As to whether I would do the same sort of house for a client, I can only say that, obviously, interests and lifestyles vary greatly; however, in large measure, given a somewhat similar program, I feel that this is the best solution for this piece of land.

"In respect to our other work, I believe that the house does demonstrate the ability of a well considered design to optimize a piece of land which, to the conventional prespective, has no feasibility at all. I think it is a case where adversity became almost an asset."

A very different house, created in spite of very different kinds of adversity, is the home of a husband-and-wife team of architects, Barbara and Allan Anderson (page 222). They too tell a story that is fun to read, and that shows that the dreams of many young families—of a fine house on a limited budget—can at least sometimes come true:

"The idea for our house evolved after spending a number of months of week ends looking for an old house to fix up in Westchester and finding nothing but rabbit warrens and decay. One afternoon while looking at a Splanch [split-level ranch] we spotted the leftover rocky forested site next to Mead Pond. We found that its cost was very small, due to the apparent difficulties presented by the rocky outcropping. No stock plans could be used here. We decided we could afford a house if we could build it ourselves.

"Knowing that we had only week ends to work and a small budget, we stuck to simple shed construction, using commonly available stock parts from the local lumber yards, which we could buy as we went along.

"We reacted to years in a tiny apartment, wanting privacy but openness. This resulted in the three almost separate but open elements: the children's area, the adults' area, and the common open living and entertaining area, all forming a private court.

"With only amateur help from friends and relatives, space, light, proportion and stock parts had to be our design elements. No elaborate details could be afforded, nor did we have the mechanics to execute them.

"The rocky leftover piece of land was in itself a challenge. We spent five months of hand labor excavating the foundations to bedrock. The beauty of the existing ecology was also thereby preserved, leaving us with natural gardens of oaks, huckleberries, azalea and viburnum, untouched by machinery.

"Some of our design problems related to being the last house in an existing neighborhood. We felt that sloped roofs would tie in better with the existing gable houses, and we chose bleached cedar for the exterior to blend in with the grays of the oaks and the rocks. Privacy was achieved by avoiding windows towards the neighbors and setting the house back in a corner looking out over the pond.

"This is exactly the approach I would take for other people with minimum means, and in fact I have been asked a number of times to repeat the design with variations for other people.

"The economic constraints, perhaps, have made this one of our most successful projects—in that it is the least mannered. Simplicity can produce a serenity appropriate to residential environs. Three design awards attest to others feeling the same way.

"This adventure in low-cost housing 'the hard way' gave us an opportunity to learn by doing all the basic crafts and skills. For my wife, since the profession normally excludes women from this experience, the process was a unique education. Being architect, owner and contractor at the same time gave us much freedom for experimentation within economic constraints, and the process was a joy to experience."

The Moore House

Architects who like building puzzles will understand why Arthur Moore had such fun getting his own house in Georgetown built. On a 2,150-square-foot site that sloped steeply, he worked five years on a design that satisfied two very conservative fine arts commissions and the zoning board, yet met the Moores' needs for a spacious and completely private residence. The exterior (top left) was largely imposed by the governing bodies when they insisted the house be built to the limits of the lot (80-foot frontage and 4 feet wide at the point) and that it have a mansard roof. But behind that facade—wow!

The Moores wanted as large a swimming pool and as large a living room as possible. Both were achieved by overhanging the former with the latter. The structure, says Moore, is not terribly clear but it works. In fact, every detail works and with a sense of humor that makes this truly architects' architecture. The diagonal steel angles on the rear elevation, for instance, will eventually support an awning fastened above the mirrored pool edge. Voila, an enclosed heated pool! The bubble window then becomes the only way to observe the back of the house, including the tent. In the point on the second floor, the Moores have a huge sunken tub to which, at present, guests repair when rain spoils swimming parties. The entire house, in short, is a celebration of a life style to which many architects no doubt aspire. Arthur Moore had not only the vision but the will to achieve it.

Architect and *owner:* Arthur Cotton Moore. *Location:* Georgetown, Washington, D.C. *Engineers:* Milton A. Gurewitz and Associates (structural); Cotton and Harris (mechanical & electrical). *Contractor:* Coleman and Wood.

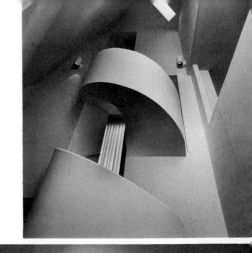

A sinuous winding stair is the core of the Moore house. After one has entered—confronting the pool head on—a clever reverse stair and landing starts one up the spiral. The spacious living room made more so by the compact built-in couch, has complete privacy from nearby neighbors even though one wall is completely glazed. A series of five panes let into the rafters light the piano, which is the only other piece of furniture in the room.

Norman C. McGrath photos

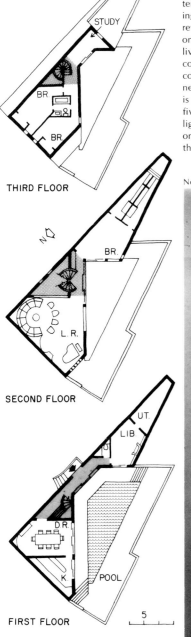

THIRD FLOOR

SECOND FLOOR

FIRST FLOOR

5

The three-part plan was derived from careful study of the site. The section indicates how little the existing rock profile was modified to accommodate the various levels.

The Anderson House

This house cost $21,000 in 1971, because architects Allan and Barbara Anderson designed and built it themselves. And perhaps even more important, the completed house blends into its rocky site so well that it is almost invisible in summer to its split-level neighbors.

For the Andersons, it was an adventure and an education that any architect would envy. The 2¼-acre parcel had been on the market in Rye, New York for many years. Since one-third of it is under a pond, one-third right-of-way and one-third a 30-foot-high rockpile adjacent to the pond, it is no surprise that the price was very reasonable. The property is covered with mature oaks and a wide variety of other plant life, and the Andersons made an especially careful survey and topographic model. The scheme, as developed from that, threads its way around the rocks and oaks, and opens out into the environment in every direction. Since very little of the existing ecology was damaged—it took them five months of hard-labor weekends to pin the foundations to the rocks as they found them—complete privacy and a sense of wilderness, in the midst of suburbia, has been maintained.

A single roof plane (photo and section, right) sweeps from the ridge high on the rocks down toward the pond. It is interrupted only by a contraposed shed which shelters a living room balcony set into the main roof. At the upper end of the house (right), a series of smaller-scale shed roofs provide light and interesting interior space for bedrooms and the study where the two architects work side-by-side. "It was a rare opportunity," says Allan Anderson, "to learn by doing. And for my wife, in an area normally excluded to women by the profession—the building experience—it was uniquely valuable."

Architects, owners, engineers, interior designers and contractors: Barbara and Allan Anderson. Location: Rye, New York.

Ezra Stoller © ESTO photos

SECTION A-A

The living and dining spaces both under the sweep of the main roof, each overlook the pond. From the kitchen which separates them, one can share in living room activity, yet the distraction of cooking is thoroughly hidden from guests. All built-in cabinet work is by the Andersons. The bedrooms and study have high ceilings and vistas up into the surrounding oaks.

INDEX